DAN TOOMBS

THE CURRY GUY EASY

100 fuss-free British Indian Restaurant classics to make at home

Photography by Kris Kirkham

quadrille

For Caroline, Katy,
Joe & Jennifer

PREFACE

This cookbook celebrates over 100 of my favourite, easy curry house recipes that I cook all the time at home. These are recipes that represent the best of the British curry house, past, present and future. You might be surprised to learn that many of the recipes in this book have been served at curry houses for decades, but are only now catching on with the general public. Our tastes and expectations are changing and the best chefs are stepping up to the mark to ensure we are not disappointed.

When I set about writing a cookbook of 'easy' curry house recipes, it took some time for me to get my head around exactly what 'easy' meant. Curry house-style cooking was, after all, developed over the decades for ease, efficiency and economy. In British curry houses, there is a bit of prep work to do to get the recipes right, but few would consider the tasks difficult. Still, I knew there must be a way to get around doing some of the more tedious jobs without compromising on flavour. I think I've done it with this book!

It's little wonder, with all the long lists of ingredients and perhaps unfamiliar cooking techniques, that many people find the idea of whipping up an Indian feast somewhat daunting. The thing is, many of the ingredients are used in varying amounts in almost every recipe and the techniques really aren't that difficult. With the exception of some of the more speciality ingredients I have listed on page 155, you will probably already have what you need on hand. The majority of the ingredients required for these recipes can easily be sourced at your local supermarket.

If you have a copy of my first book *The Curry Guy: Recreate over 100 of the best British Indian restaurant recipes at home*, you will probably know that one of the most important recipes in curry house cooking is the famous base curry sauce. I have featured another authentic version in this book, but have also included a cheat's recipe so that you can cook the sauce in minutes! My new quick and easy base sauce (see page 50) will get you cooking amazing curry house-style curries in no time! Many chefs, however, no longer use or have never used a base curry sauce, opting to cook in a more traditional 'home-style'.

I have included information so that you can choose the cooking style you prefer or find easiest.

There was no way I wanted to compromise on taste by cutting corners just to make these recipes easy. I wanted the recipes to taste just as good as the dishes you will find at your favourite local curry house. If anything, they had to be better so that you would have a good reason to stay in and cook. So I have focused on what it is that we all want when we go out for a curry. There was a time when going out to our local Indian restaurant meant ordering a good chicken tikka masala, korma, jalfrezi or phaal, together with a few eagerly selected side dishes and a pint or three to wash it all down. For many, these classic curry house dishes are still top of the list, which is why I included so many of the old favourites in my first book. For others, going out is all about experiencing something new and exciting, just like the above mentioned curries were different and exciting back in their day.

Hopefully you will already have a copy of my first book and can refer to it for information on making my homemade spice blends and other base ingredients and pastes. I have written this book so that you can continue the journey and use it alongside the first. If you don't have a copy, no worries! All of the recipes featured here can be made with good-quality shop-bought spice blends and main ingredients. It just didn't feel right wasting book space with recipes I had already published. Besides, most busy curry houses use commercially available spice masalas and pastes, so you will get recognizable and delicious results using these recipes even if you decide to do the same.

I hope you enjoy cooking from this cookbook as much as I have enjoyed developing and serving the recipes to my family and friends. Cooking is my passion so please don't be a stranger. I am on Twitter and Facebook almost daily (@TheCurryGuy) and I'd love to hear from you. I'm happy to help you with any recipe questions you may have.

Happy Cooking!
Dan

HOW TO USE THIS COOKBOOK

One of the things I loved most when my first book was published was getting to know so many people, both online and at events. The feedback I received about that book was invaluable!

So many people I met loved the way they could take a few hours to do the forward preparation required to make curry house-style food and then easily whip up a curry in minutes whenever they wanted one. Of course I enjoyed getting that feedback but there was another group who wanted to make an Indian meal but didn't want to do all the preparation. Put simply, they didn't consider the recipes easy if they had to prepare other recipes to get started with the one they wanted to make.

I knew I needed to make the recipes in this book easy, regardless of what you consider to be easy. For this reason, I have labelled each recipe with what is required to make it, along with dietary information, so that you can see at a glance which is right for you. If you want something quick and easy, look for the '30 minutes or less' badges. If you want a fuss-free recipe but have a little more time, look for the 'low and slow' badges. The following labels will help you find the recipes that best suit your requirements.

DON'T BE HOSTAGE TO THE RECIPES!
My goal with this book is to make it possible for you to cook recipes just like they do at the best British curry houses. Explanations on how to do this are in every recipe but please don't feel like you have to do exactly as I say. The most important thing in cooking delicious food is using the best-quality ingredients you can find. Everything else can be tailored to your own requirements. Pre-cooked meat, for example is called for in the classic British curries section (see pages 48 –71). Adding pre-cooked meat is done at restaurants for speed and flavour. Using the tender cooked meat and cooking stock in these curries will speed up the cooking time but if you don't have any prepared, you can still make the recipes. Just add the meat raw but remember, this may increase cooking times substantially as red meat needs to slowly simmer for 40–60 minutes to become tender. Just add water or stock as needed and don't rush it.

In the end, you have a magnificent curry. For the novice cook, the most important thing to remember is that very little can go wrong. Feel free to tweak these recipes to your own taste. If you think I have used more chilli powder than you will be comfortable with, reduce or omit it completely. If you want your curry spicier, add more chilli powder or fresh chillies. The same holds true for all of the ingredients.

RECIPE LABELS

 30 mins or less: Look for this icon when you just want something quick and easy.

 Low and slow: Longer cooking times are required but the preparation is simple.

 Marinating or fermenting time required: For optimum flavour, you will need to marinate/ferment the ingredients before cooking the recipe.

 Gluten free: Most of the recipes in this book are gluten free or can easily be made gluten free. Look for the badge.

 Vegetarian: I have included many of my favourite vegetarian recipes. To find them, just look for this badge.

 BIR: BIR or 'British Indian Restaurant' is a term most often used to describe British-style curries. These recipes call for the use of a base curry sauce (see pages 50 and 51 for base sauce recipes) and often pre-cooked meat, poultry and vegetables.

Perfect for the barbecue: Spot this badge and the recipe can be made in a conventional oven but tastes even better done on the barbecue.

INGREDIENT SHORTCUTS AND SUBSTITUTES

Fresh is usually best, but sometimes it's nice to know you can cheat a bit. Following are some of my suggestions that will save you time and, in some cases, money.

Chopped onions: If you are short on time or simply don't like runny eyes from chopping onions, purchase them pre-chopped from the supermarket. They work fine but it's, of course, cheaper to chop your own.

Crispy fried onions: I usually fry my own sliced onions until crispy brown. You can purchase crispy fried onions if you wish. They work really well in curries and marinades. You will get a lot more for your money purchasing fried onions in the large bags from Asian shops.

Onion paste: Onion paste is made by frying thinly sliced onions until crispy and brown, then blending them with just enough water or yoghurt to make a thick paste. You can use shop-bought crispy fried onions to save time and make less mess. You can add a little onion paste to many curries for additional flavour, even if the recipe doesn't call for it.

Mixed garlic and ginger paste: Garlic and ginger paste is so easy to make. Simply peel equal amounts of garlic and ginger and blend with just enough water to make a paste. If this sounds like a bit too much work, you can also purchase it ready made at Asian grocers and most supermarkets. You can also substitute grated or finely chopped garlic and ginger for the blended paste. Some stores only stock garlic paste and ginger paste in separate jars. Just take equal amounts of both out and mix them to make the garlic and ginger paste needed for most recipes in this book.

Rice: It really couldn't be easier to cook perfect rice, as you will see from my recipe on page 149. It's just a matter of soaking the rice, placing it in a pan with the right amount of water, bringing it to a boil and letting it steam for 40 minutes. There is now good-quality cooked rice available and it works really well. I have been known to use pouches of ready-cooked basmati rice when I want to cheat a bit.

Tomato purée: Tomato purée is called for in many curries. For ease, I have recommended using plain passata (sieved tomatoes) or blended canned tomatoes in the following recipes. You can also make it by whisking one part thick tomato paste with three parts water.

Rice flour: I use rice flour in many recipes. It is gluten free and really helps make fried food extra crispy. You can substitute cornflour (cornstarch) if you have trouble finding it. Likewise, if you are looking for a gluten-free flour to use instead of cornflour, rice flour works really well. Rice flour is available at Asian grocers, online and also in many larger supermarkets.

Methi leaves (fenugreek leaves): Kasuri methi (dried fenugreek leaves) and fresh methi are available at most Asian grocers. Dried is easier to come by than fresh. When asking for them in an Asian shop, don't ask for fenugreek leaves as you will probably get a blank stare in return. If all you can find is dried kasuri methi, it can be substituted for fresh. I suggest stirring in the dried leaves to taste at the end of cooking. A good alternative to using dried or fresh methi are chopped celery leaves. They have a similar, but not as bitter, flavour to fenugreek. Another option would be to use a handful or two of chopped spinach with some ground fenugreek. This will give the look and flavour of using fresh fenugreek leaves. Remember, though, fenugreek is bitter and can quickly become overpowering. Add dried fenugreek in small $1/2$ teaspoon amounts to taste.

STARTERS

The following recipes are hugely popular at Indian restaurants and usually appear in the starters section. Don't feel like you have to serve them as starters though. They are all delicious and make perfect main courses too.

(GF)

Chicken wings are becoming a popular starter at lots of Indian restaurants. You might have seen many delicious options, from spicy garlic salt to Portuguese piri piri. They may not all be flavoured with the ingredients you would expect at a curry house, but I've never heard anyone complain! This is a recipe I developed after picking some chicken wings up at a food festival. The chef was happy to tell me what went into his marinade and I think I got it just right.

Usually chicken is served skinned at Indian restaurants. Skinned chicken wings are available from most halal butchers. I tried skinning them myself once and won't again. It was way too much work. Of course unskinned chicken wings are a lot fattier but the crispy chicken skin is worth every calorie.

SWEET AND SPICY CHICKEN WINGS
SERVES 4 OR MORE AS PART OF A MULTI-COURSE MEAL

PREP TIME: 15 MINUTES, PLUS MARINATING
COOKING TIME: 40 MINUTES

1kg (2lb 2oz) chicken wings, preferably skinned
3 tbsp roasted hot pepper sauce (see page 143) or shop-bought chilli sauce
Raita, to serve

FOR THE MARINADE
2 tbsp garlic and ginger paste (see page 7)
1 tbsp green chilli paste (or 2–3 green chillies, finely chopped)
1 tsp tamarind concentrate
2 tbsp cider vinegar
3 tbsp Worcestershire sauce
4 tbsp honey
1 tsp chilli powder (or to taste)
1 tbsp ground cumin
Juice of 3 limes
Salt and freshly ground black pepper

Mix all the marinade ingredients in a large bowl. Add the chicken wings and coat well with the marinade. Leave to marinate for 2 hours, or up to 48 hours.

When ready to cook, preheat your oven to 200°C/400°F/Gas 6. Arrange the marinated chicken wings on a lightly greased baking tray and place on the middle rack. Cook for about 30 minutes and then give the chicken a good shake and cook for another 10 minutes, or until cooked through and slightly blackened on the outside. Stir in the hot sauce and serve with a good raita like the spicy coriander raita on page 139.

I'm asked often why this dish is called 'Chicken 65'. There is no one definite answer, but there are two explanations which I think are better than most. One is that the original recipe had 65 different ingredients in it. More likely is that in India, where the menus can be very long and people order by number, this dish began showing up as the sixty-fifth option on numerous menus, making it easy to go out and order the very popular number 65 without even looking at the menu. The deep frying in this recipe can be done ahead of time, so if you are serving this curry house classic to dinner guests, you won't need to be standing over hot oil when everyone arrives.

CHICKEN 65
SERVES 6 OR MORE AS PART OF A MULTI-COURSE MEAL

PREP TIME: 20 MINUTES, PLUS MARINATING
COOKING TIME: 10 MINUTES

1kg (2lb 2oz) chicken breasts
Rapeseed oil, for deep frying
1 tsp black mustard seeds
1 tsp cumin seeds
20 curry leaves (see page 155)
3 green chillies, sliced
12 garlic cloves, finely chopped
10cm (4in) piece of ginger, julienned
3 spring onions (scallions), roughly chopped
2 tbsp lemon juice
2–3 tbsp roasted hot pepper sauce (see page 143) or shop-bought chilli sauce (optional)

FOR THE SPICED BATTER
2 eggs, beaten
2 tbsp mixed garlic and ginger paste (see page 7)
3 tbsp cornflour (cornstarch)
3 tbsp rice flour (see page 155)
1 tsp ground turmeric
1 tbsp ground cumin
1 tsp ground coriander
2 tsp chilli powder
1½ tbsp tandoori masala
1 tsp salt
1 tbsp freshly ground black pepper

Slice the chicken breasts into small bite-sized pieces (tikka). Mix all the batter ingredients into a paste, then rub it evenly into the chicken pieces. If time permits, let this marinate for about 30 minutes or overnight, but this isn't crucial.

When ready to deep fry, heat your oil in a large wok. The oil should be at least 10cm (4in) deep. The oil is ready when a small piece of chicken sizzles immediately upon putting it in the oil. If using an oil thermometer, aim for 190°C/375°F.

Fry the chicken in batches until the exterior is nice and crispy and the meat is almost cooked through. This should take about 2–3 minutes per batch. Place the finished chicken pieces on a wire rack to rest while you fry the remaining batches. The frying can be done ahead of time. Store the fried chicken, covered in the fridge until ready to use.

Once cooled a bit, remove all but about 3 tablespoons of the oil from the wok. Place over high heat and toss in the mustard seeds. When they begin to pop, reduce the heat to medium–high, add the cumin seeds, curry leaves and green chillies and fry for a further 30 seconds. Stir in the garlic and ginger and fry until fragrant and soft – about 1 minute should do the job.

Tip in the chicken and spring onions (scallions) and stir well to coat. Fry it all over high heat until the chicken is completely cooked through. Squeeze the lemon juice over the top and add the hot pepper sauce, if using. Give it all one last good stir, check for seasoning, adding a little more salt if needed, and serve.

This British curry house classic is hugely popular and also quick and easy to make. I like to add shallow-fried tandoori chicken (see page 15) or any of the grilled (broiled) chicken recipes in this book as the smoky flavour really adds to the dish. You could really add any leftover cooked chicken. It's a great way of giving new life to your leftover Sunday dinner chicken roast! You can also cook the chicken from raw. Just cut the raw chicken into bite-sized pieces and be sure to cook it through in the sauce.

CHICKEN CHAAT

SERVES 4 OR MORE AS PART OF A MULTI-COURSE MEAL

PREP TIME: 10 MINUTES
COOKING TIME: 20 MINUTES

3 tbsp rapeseed oil
1 onion, finely chopped
2 tbsp mixed garlic and ginger
    paste (see page 7)
2 tbsp mixed powder
    (see page 49) or curry powder
1 tsp chilli powder
2 tbsp chaat masala (see
    page 155)
150ml (^{2}/$_3$ cup) tomato purée
    (see page 7)
400ml (1^3/$_4$ cups) base curry
    sauce (see pages 50 or 51)
700g (1lb 9oz) pre-cooked
    chicken (see page 34)
^{1}/$_2$ cucumber, peeled, deseeded
    and cut into 2.5cm (1in)
    pieces
^{1}/$_2$ red pepper (bell pepper),
    roughly chopped
100g (3^1/$_2$oz) drained canned
    chickpeas (garbanzo beans)
1 large tomato, cut into 8 wedges
1 tsp garam masala
Salt

Heat the oil in a frying pan over medium–high heat. When it's visibly hot, add the chopped onion. Stir the onion around in the oil for a couple of minutes until soft and translucent. Add the garlic and ginger paste and give it all another good stir.

Spoon in the mixed powder or curry powder, chilli powder and chaat masala, followed by the tomato purée. This should sizzle when it hits the pan. When it does, add half the base curry sauce. Allow this to bubble for a minute or so, only stirring if the sauce begins to stick to the pan. Add the chicken pieces and the rest of the stock and simmer until the chicken is cooked through – about 10 minutes should do the job.

To finish, stir in the cucumber, (bell) pepper, chickpeas (garbanzo beans) and tomato wedges. Add salt to taste and sprinkle with the garam masala.

 (GF)

Smoky charred tandoori chicken is delicious served on its own or added to a curry like chicken tikka masala. Using my charcoal method, you will achieve the taste of the tandoor while cooking in a frying pan. Adding the charcoal is optional so if it sounds a bit too much like hard work, leave out that step. If you would rather cook in the oven, simply place the marinated chicken on a wire rack in an oven that has been pre-heated to 200°C/400°F and roast until cooked through, turning once. If using a meat thermometer, aim for 75–80°C/167–176°F.

SHALLOW-FRIED TANDOORI CHICKEN

SERVES 4

PREP TIME: 10–20 MINUTES, PLUS MARINATING
COOKING TIME: 15 MINUTES, PLUS SMOKING

8 chicken thighs, skinned
Juice of 1 lemon
Salt
1–2 pieces of charcoal (optional)
3 generous tbsp ghee or
   rapeseed oil
1/2 tsp garam masala
1 onion, thinly sliced
2 limes, quartered

FOR THE MARINADE
200g (scant 1 cup) Greek yoghurt
1 tbsp cream cheese
1 tbsp rapeseed oil
1 tsp ground turmeric
1 tbsp ground cumin
1 tsp ground coriander
1 tbsp red chilli powder
1 tbsp tandoori masala
2 tbsp mixed garlic and ginger
   paste (see page 7)
Salt

Use a sharp knife to make 3 shallow incisions in each chicken thigh, put them in a bowl and mix with the lemon juice and 3/4 teaspoon salt.

Whisk all of the marinade ingredients together until you have a smooth emulsion. If you don't mind getting your hands dirty, this can be done by hand. Pour the marinade over the chicken and rub it into the flesh and slits. Cover with cling film (plastic wrap) and marinate for at least 30 minutes or overnight in the fridge.

When ready to cook, light two pieces of charcoal and let them turn white hot. This step should be done outdoors and is optional.

Melt the ghee in a frying pan with a tight-fitting lid over medium–high heat. When visibly hot, place the chicken pieces in the pan. Don't overcrowd your pan as the chicken will release water and it won't char correctly. (Fry in batches if necessary.) Fry on the first side for about 2 minutes, then turn them over and fry on the opposite side for another 2 minutes until you have a nice charred crust on both sides. Reduce the heat if needed and continue frying for about 8 more minutes, turning from time to time, until cooked through.

Move the cooked chicken to the sides of the pan, leaving a well in the centre. Carefully transfer the charcoal to a piece of silver foil and lower it into the centre of the pan. Drizzle about a teaspoon of oil on the charcoal and it will start smoking heavily.

Cover the pan and let the chicken smoke for about 5 minutes, or until the smoke has died down inside. Garnish a warmed plate with the sliced onion and lime quarters add the chicken, season with salt to taste and serve.

I absolutely love this chaat! The green mint and mango sauce and the tamarind sauce can be purchased from most good Asian grocers or online. If you fancy a go at making your own, I have included recipes on pages 145 and 146. Rice flakes (phoa) are also available at Asian shops. You could leave them out but they really do help give the aloo tikki an amazing crispy texture.

ALOO TIKKI CHAAT

SERVES 4–8

PREP TIME: 10 MINUTES
COOKING TIME: 20 MINUTES
PLUS THE TIME IT TAKES TO
PAR-COOK POTATOES

250g (1 cup) Greek yoghurt
1 tsp chaat masala (see page 155)
½ tsp red chilli powder
Juice of 1 lime
4 medium potatoes, unpeeled
4 heaped tbsp rice flour
4 heaped tbsp phoa (rice flakes,
   see page 155), soaked in
   2 tbsp water for 30 minutes
   (optional)
Rapeseed or vegetable oil, for
   frying
A pinch of asafoetida (see
   page 155)
½ tsp cumin seeds
3 green chillies, finely chopped
2.5cm (1in) piece of ginger,
   finely chopped
1 tsp ground coriander
½ tsp ground turmeric
½ tsp chilli powder
1 small bunch of coriander
   (cilantro), finely chopped
Salt
Mango and mint sauce
   (see page 146), to serve
Tamarind sauce (see page 145),
   to serve

Whisk the yoghurt for about 2 minutes until airy and light. Stir in the chaat masala, chilli powder and lime juice and season with salt to taste. Set aside.

Boil the potatoes in their skins until almost tender, but still with a little resistance when a knife is inserted. Allow to cool a little, then peel and grate the potatoes into a mixing bowl. Stir in the rice flour. Squeeze any excess liquid from the soaked rice flakes, if using, and add them too.

In a small frying pan, heat about 2 tablespoons oil over medium–high heat until hot. Add the asafoetida and cumin seeds to the hot oil and fry for about 30 seconds, then add the chillies and ginger. Fry for a further minute or so, then stir in the ground coriander, turmeric and chilli powder.

Sauté until the chillies and ginger are cooked through – about 2 minutes should be enough – then remove from the heat to cool slightly. Pour this mixture and the chopped coriander (cilantro) into the bowl with the grated potatoes and mix well by hand. Season with salt to taste.

Mash the mixture lightly with a potato masher or by hand. The mixture shouldn't be completely mashed and you should still be able to see that the potatoes have been grated. Form the mixture into golf ball-sized balls, then press down on them gently to form them into patties (tikki).

Shallow fry the tikki in about 2.5cm (1in) hot oil for 2 minutes on one side, then flip over to fry the other side for 2 minutes. If needed, fry for a little more time to brown to your preferred colour. Season with salt to taste and top generously with the yoghurt mixture and the mango and tamarind sauces.

30

Whenever I'm in Glasgow, I have to order haggis pakoras. I've been told that is where they originated, though I haven't been able to confirm it. One thing I like about haggis pakoras is that they are so British. You wouldn't find anything like these in the Indian subcontinent. Whoever it was that invented haggis pakoras must have known that they were on to a good thing. Take a product that is loved all over Scotland and the rest of Britain and give it a deep fried, spicy Indian touch. Genius!

This recipe was sent to me by my friend Monir Mohammed, cookbook author and owner of several popular restaurants including Glasgow's The Wee Curry Shop, where these haggis pakoras are very popular. Vegetarian haggis can be substituted if you wish.

HAGGIS PAKORAS
SERVES 4 OR MORE AS PART OF A MULTI-COURSE MEAL

PREP TIME: 10 MINUTES
COOKING TIME: 10 MINUTES

Rapeseed, vegetable or
    sunflower oil, for frying
450g (1lb) haggis, cut into 4cm
    (1½in) cubes
Salt
Raita, chutney and hot sauce
    (see page 139–41) or shop
    bought, to serve

FOR THE BATTER
150g (heaped 1 cup) gram
    (chickpea) flour
50g (½ cup) cornflour
    (cornstarch)
1 tbsp salt
1 tbsp red chilli powder
¼ tsp ground turmeric
1 tsp cumin seeds, toasted
1 tsp coriander seeds, toasted

Start by preparing your batter. Sift the gram flour and cornflour (cornstarch) into a large bowl and add the salt and all the spices. Add 150ml (⅔ cup) water and whisk everything together until you get a smooth batter.

Heat about 10cm (4in) depth of oil in a large pan or wok. The oil is hot enough when a little bit of the batter sizzles immediately when dripped into the oil. If you have a cooking thermometer, aim for 190°C/375°F.

Dip the haggis cubes in the batter and cook in batches until golden and crisp. About 2 minutes per batch should do the job, but only take the pakora out when they have a nice crispy brown crust. Transfer the cooked pakoras to a paper towel and keep them warm while you cook the rest in the same way. Season with salt and serve with lemon wedges, raita, chutney and/or hot sauce.

This is Bangladeshi comfort food that is delicious as a starter or snack. You can find Asian vermicelli at Asian grocers and online. Feel free to use Italian vermicelli if you have trouble finding the Asian stuff. Asian vermicelli is quite a lot finer. When cooked, the fine pasta tends to clump together, but that is one of the things that makes it more interesting and different from the Italian.

BANGLADESHI VERMICELLI
SERVES 4

PREP TIME: 5 MINUTES
COOKING TIME: 10 MINUTES

150g (5¹/₂oz) Asian vermicelli
3 tbsp rapeseed oil
1 onion, finely chopped
2 green chillies, finely chopped
2 garlic cloves, finely sliced
¹/₂ tsp ground turmeric
¹/₂ tsp curry powder
2 eggs
3 tbsp chopped coriander
   (cilantro)
Salt
Lemon wedges, to serve

Bring a pot of water to a boil and add the vermicelli. It only needs to cook for 3–4 minutes as it is so thin. When cooked, pour it into a colander and rinse with cold water.

Heat the oil in the pan you used to cook the vermicelli over medium–high heat. When visibly hot, add the chopped onion and fry until soft and lightly browned. Add the green chillies and garlic slivers and fry for a further 1 minute or so.

Add the turmeric and curry powder followed by the eggs and fry it all up until good and scrambled.

Tip in the cooked vermicelli and toss it around until well mixed and heated through.

Season with salt to taste, sprinkle with the coriander (cilantro) and squeeze lemon juice, to taste, over the top to serve.

GF

Put simply, Indo-Chinese fusion food just plain gets it and I love this Chinese-Indian combo. The recipe calls for using your favourite shop-bought chilli sauce, but you could also try making my recipe on page 143. The cooking time for this one is a bit long, but there is really very little work to do.

When we cooked these during the photo shoot for this book, they went down a treat! We were running short on time but they were so good we decided to make another batch. I'm telling you... this sweet and sour chicken is addictive!

INDO-CHINESE
SWEET AND SOUR CHICKEN
SERVES 4 OR MORE AS PART OF A MULTI-COURSE MEAL

PREP TIME: 20 MINUTES
COOKING TIME: 1 HOUR

1kg (2lb 2oz) boneless and skinless chicken thighs, cut into thirds
Garlic salt, to taste
$1/2$ tsp amchoor (dried mango powder, see page 155)
Cornflour (cornstarch) or rice flour (see page 155), for dusting
Oil, for browning the chicken
100g ($1/2$ cup) sugar
125ml ($1/2$ cup) vinegar
2 tbsp red chilli hot sauce
4 tbsp ketchup
1 tbsp dark soy sauce or coconut amino (see page 155)
65ml ($1/4$ cup) orange juice
Salt and freshly ground black pepper

Preheat the oven to 175°C/350°F/Gas 4 and line a baking pan with foil or baking parchment to make clearing up easier.

Sprinkle the chicken pieces with garlic salt, to taste, and the amchoor powder and set aside for about 10 minutes. Meanwhile, heat about 2.5cm (1in) depth of oil in a saucepan set over medium–high heat. Roll the chicken pieces in cornflour (cornstarch) to coat well, then fry them in the oil for about 3 minutes, or until lightly browned. Set aside.

Mix together the sugar, vinegar, chilli sauce, ketchup, soy sauce or coconut amino and orange juice with a dash of salt and pepper in a saucepan. Over medium–high heat, stir the sauce until the sugar has dissolved.

Place a single layer of the chicken on the prepared baking tray and pour the sauce over. Bake for 1 hour until browned and crispy. For best results you will need to turn the chicken pieces a few times during cooking, but I often forget and have never been disappointed.

Transfer the cooked chicken to a serving plate and serve, or just serve in the tray! It will save you washing up and I really don't think anyone will complain.

This is a nice one for breakfast, lunch, dinner or snack time. It can be made in minutes and is delicious spread over naans or French bread. This recipe has been adapted from a recipe sent to me by my friend Eshan (Mo) Miah, owner of Zahman's in Newquay. When I tried it, I knew it had to be in this book!

BHAJA MACKEREL
SERVES 2

PREP TIME: 5 MINUTES
COOKING TIME: 10 MINUTES

2 tbsp rapeseed oil
1/2 onion, finely chopped
3 green chillies, finely chopped
200g (7oz) fresh tomatoes, chopped
1 egg
250g (9oz) smoked mackerel
1/2 tsp ground cumin
1/2 tsp paprika
1/2 tsp ground coriander
3 tbsp finely chopped coriander (cilantro)
Salt and freshly ground black pepper

Heat a frying pan over medium heat and add the rapeseed oil. Throw in the chopped onion and green chilli peppers. Fry, stirring from time to time, until the onion is soft and light brown in colour. Tip in the chopped tomatoes and stir to combine.

Now add the egg and smoked mackerel and stir into the other ingredients, breaking the fish fillet as you do. When everything looks good and scrambled, add the cumin, paprika, ground coriander and fresh chopped coriander (cilantro). Season with salt and pepper to taste and serve immediately.

(GF) (V)

I've loved pani puris for years but it wasn't until I met Pratik Master, owner of the excellent restaurant Lilu in Leicester, that it dawned on me how easily these delicious flavour bombs could be served at home. Pratik prepared a plate of puri shells with a variety of easy-to-make fillings and we sat, snacked and chatted for hours.

Making the small puri shells is difficult and therefore beyond the scope of an easy cookbook, but you can purchase them ready made at Asian grocers and online. Good-quality black and green pani (water) can also be purchased but I have included recipes for both on pages 144 and 145 if you want to make your own.

Get everything prepared ahead of time and let your friends go wild on filling their puris.

PANI PURI
SERVES 6–12

PREP TIME: 15 MINUTES
COOKING TIME: 20 MINUTES
FOR THE POTATO

400g (14oz) can chickpeas
  (garbanzo beans), drained
150g (5½oz) room temperature
  boiled potato, grated or cut
  into very small pieces
30 small puri shells

LITTLE EXTRAS FOR SERVING
Salt
Chilli powder
Ground cumin
2 lemons, cut into wedges
Amchor (dried mango powder,
  see page 155)
200g (¾ cup) plain yoghurt,
  whisked
Chaat masala (see page 155)
Finely chopped coriander
  (cilantro)
Pomegranate seeds
Tamarind sauce (see page 145
  or shop bought)
Green pani (see page 144
  or shop bought)
Black pani (see page 145
  or shop bought)
Fine sev or boondi (see page 155)

This is more of a fun assembly line than a recipe. Place your boiled potatoes (grated or cut) in a serving bowl. Do the same with the chickpeas. Prepare bowls of the other ingredients and/or come up with a few sides of your own. This can all be done ahead of time.

When ready, let the pani puri party commence! Present the puri shells with all the toppings and there's nothing more to do than say 'dig in'! Tell people to gently break open the top of the puri shells with their finger and try them with different fillings. Some might like them with just chickpeas, chilli powder, chaat masala, yoghurt and pomegranate seeds. Others might fill them with a bit of everything before topping the tiny puri shell with the green or black pani (water) and a good sprinkling of sev or boondi and popping them into their mouth. Don't add anything to the puri shells beforehand or the shells will get soggy.

You can really get creative with pani puris. Try them with fried potatoes or perhaps a spoonful of my 40-garlic-clove chutney (see page 139). The sky's the limit.

Mulligatawny soup stems from the Madras (Chennai) region of India but has been popular here in the UK for at least two centuries. The Indian name for Mulligatawny is 'rasam' (or pepper water) and this recipe includes a lot of black pepper! It is different to most of the Mulligatawny soups I've tried, but it's right up there with the best. The thing is, there is no one recipe for the soup, which can vary greatly in flavour and colour. This recipe was sent to me by my friend Palash Mitra, head chef of Gymkhana in London. The broken idlis you see in the soup are optional but tasty extras.

MULLIGATAWNY SOUP
SERVES 4

PREP TIME: 10 MINUTES
COOKING TIME: 30 MINUTES

25g (2 tbsp) butter
3 bay leaves
5cm (2in) cinnamon stick
6 cloves
1 large red onion, finely diced
1 stick celery, diced
1 carrot, diced
50g (1¾oz) canned plum
    tomatoes, roughly chopped
½ leek, diced
1 tbsp plain (all-purpose) flour
1 litre (cups) salt-free chicken or
    vegetable stock
400ml (14 fl oz) can of thick
    coconut milk
Salt
4 broken idlis (see page 108)
    (optional)
4 lemon wedges, to serve

FOR THE SPICE PASTE
1 tbsp ground cumin
1 tbsp ground coriander
1 tbsp freshly ground black
    pepper
1 tsp ground turmeric
6 garlic cloves, peeled
4cm (1½in) piece of ginger,
    roughly chopped
Handful each of fresh coriander
    (cilantro) and mint leaves

Put all the spice paste ingredients into a food processor or blender. Add a splash of water and blitz to a paste. Leave to one side.

Melt the butter in a large heavy-bottomed saucepan. Add the bay leaves, cinnamon and cloves and fry for a minute or so to flavour the butter. Add the chopped onion and cook for 5 minutes until soft and translucent.

Now add the celery, carrot, tomatoes and leek and cook for a further 5 minutes. Stir in the spice paste and fry for a few minutes, until fragrant. Stir in the flour followed by the chicken or vegetable stock. Cover and simmer for 15 minutes until the soup has thickened. Pour in the coconut milk and mix through. Season with salt to taste and it's ready to serve. If you prefer a creamier texture as I do, blend the soup and run it through a sieve. This is by no means necessary but I like it that way. Adjust the seasoning and add more stock if the soup is too thick.

If serving with idlis, place the idli pieces in four warmed bowls and pour the hot soup over them. Or just divide the soup into bowls and serve with lemon wedges for squeezing.

Mussels are on the menu at so many restaurants, Indian and other, but I think this simple recipe is right up there with the best of them. It just goes to show, recipes don't need to be difficult to be amazing. Many people are afraid to cook mussels because of all the horror stories out there about becoming ill from a bad one. Be sure to clean and de-beard them. When you run cold water over the mussels, they should close tightly. If they don't, discard them along with any mussels that are broken. I like to serve these mussels with freshly baked naans, but French bread is a good substitute. For a gluten-free side, try plain white rice (see page 149). Adding cream is nice but not essential.

SPICED MUSSELS COOKED IN COCONUT MILK

SERVES 4

PREP TIME: 15 MINUTES
COOKING TIME: 10 MINUTES

2 tbsp unsalted butter
1 tbsp black mustard seeds
20 curry leaves (see page 155)
4 shallots, finely chopped
3 fresh green chillies, finely chopped
2 tbsp mixed garlic and ginger paste (see page 7)
400ml (14 fl oz) can thick coconut milk
175ml (²/₃ cup) dry white wine (optional)
1kg (2lb 3oz) live mussels, de-beaded and cleaned
100ml (scant ¹/₂ cup) double (heavy) cream (optional)
A pinch of saffron, soaked in a little warm milk
A pinch of ground turmeric
1 tbsp sugar or jaggery
1 small bunch of coriander (cilantro), finely chopped
Salt and freshly ground black pepper
Bread or rice, to serve

Melt the butter in a large pan that has a tight-fitting lid over high heat. When the butter has melted, throw in the mustard seeds. They'll start to pop in about 30 seconds. This is your cue to reduce the heat to medium–high and toss in the curry leaves and chopped shallots. Fry until the shallots turn soft and translucent.

Now add the chopped chillies and the garlic and ginger paste and stir to combine. Pour in the coconut milk and wine, if using, and bring to a rolling bubble. Tip in the mussels and cover with the lid to let them steam for about 4 minutes. They are ready when the shells open. Discard any shells that don't open or are broken.

Add the cream, if using, saffron milk, turmeric and the sugar. Check for seasoning, sprinkle with the chopped coriander (cilantro) and serve immediately with bread or rice.

HOME-STYLE AND STAFF CURRIES

The first two curries in this section might just become your 'go to' recipes for many curries. I know I couldn't be without them now. Lamb masala curry (see page 35) and chicken masala curry (see page 34) are proper home-style curries like you find in so many restaurants these days. They are so versatile that super-sized karahis (Indian two-handled woks) of each are prepared before every dinner service to be served as they are or to create many of the different curries on the menu. They may be mild and simple, but this is exactly what makes them so versatile.

These are not your typical classic British curries but they can be, and often are, adapted to keep customers happy. At home-style restaurants, people often ask for the curries they know even if they aren't on the menu. I've seen everything from chicken tikka masala to red hot lamb phal made using these two curries.

They are delicious in their own right but I usually add more meat and then spoon it out to use as pre-cooked meat/poultry for the classic curries that use a base sauce (see pages 50–51). The meat freezes well for up to three months. Adding more meat also adds more depth to the sauces. You could also leave the meat/poultry out and toss potatoes into either sauce as a base for numerous vegetarian curries. Just remember that potatoes require a longer cooking time than other vegetables, so cook them through first before adding the others. Broccoli and cauliflower, for example, really only need to be added at the end of cooking to achieve a perfect al dente texture.

Both the lamb masala curry and chicken masala curry have been developed to serve eight. When I make a batch, I often reserve half to serve as it is and then use the other half to make a completely different curry. Following are two recipe ideas that I adapted from the classic BIR curry section (see pages 48– 71). Feel free to come up with a few of your own using the BIR recipes in this book or from my first book. If it sounds good, it probably will be.

Home-style meat and poultry curries are usually cooked with meat on the bone. Many chefs cook the meat off the bone due to customer demand. I'll leave that one to you.

HOME-STYLE MANGO CHICKEN CURRY – SERVES 4 OR MORE AS PART OF A MULTI-COURSE MEAL

You will use one half of the chicken masala curry on page 34 for this recipe. Heat 2 tablespoons rapeseed oil in a frying pan over medium–high heat. When visibly hot, stir in 1 tablespoon mixed garlic and ginger paste (see page 7) and let it fry for about 30 seconds. Add 1 teaspoon chilli powder, along with 3 tablespoons finely chopped coriander (cilantro) stalks and two finely chopped fresh chillies. Stir really well, then add 6 tablespoons coconut flour and 4 tablespoons mango chutney, followed by your prepared chicken masala curry. I usually add this one ladleful at a time so there is less mess. Bring to a simmer and then add small or large chunks of mango from one small mango. Let the curry cook for another 4 minutes or so until it has reduced down to your preferred consistency and the mango is cooked to your liking. Check for seasoning and garnish with chopped coriander (cilantro) leaves.

HOME-STYLE LAMB ACHARI – SERVES 4 OR MORE AS PART OF A MULTI-COURSE MEAL

You will use one half of the lamb masala curry on page 35 for this recipe. Heat 2 tablespoons rapeseed oil in a frying pan over medium–high heat. When the oil is visibly hot, add 1 tablespoon panch poran (see page 155) and 2 dried Kashmiri chillies. The panch poran will begin to crackle as the spices release their flavour. Toss in one finely sliced onion and fry until soft and translucent. Add 1 tablespoon mixed garlic and ginger paste (see page 7) and 2 finely chopped bird's eye chillies and fry for a further 30 seconds while stirring. Add 1 teaspoon chilli powder (optional) and the prepared lamb masala curry one ladleful at a time. Bring to a simmer. Reduce down to your preferred consistency and then stir in 1 tablespoon lime pickle and 1 tablespoon smooth mango chutney. To finish, stir in 4 tablespoons plain yoghurt one tablespoon at a time. Sprinkle 1 teaspoon each of dried methi (fenugreek leaves) and garam masala over the top followed by the juice of one lemon. Garnish with chopped coriander (cilantro).

This is such a good recipe to have as part of your Indian curry repertoire. If you've ever ordered the 'chicken curry' off the menu at a home-style restaurant, there is a good chance it was just like this.

Although this chicken curry is delicious served as described, you can do so much more with it if you want to get creative. You could add a few handfuls of freshly chopped or frozen spinach leaves and transform this into a mouthwatering chicken saag curry. Why not try adding some thick coconut milk or whisked plain yoghurt? You'll get two different and equally tasty curries! If you like your curries spicy, a few finely chopped green bird's eye chillies and/or a couple of teaspoons of Mr Naga chilli paste, which is used at most curry houses and is available at Asian grocers and online. It will definitely turn up the heat.

On page 154 (in the bottom-left corner), I am cooking up a large batch of chicken masala curry. The smaller karahis on top are single-serving curries made with the masala curries.

CHICKEN MASALA CURRY
SERVES 8 OR MORE AS PART OF A MULTI-COURSE MEAL

PREP TIME: 10 MINUTES
COOKING TIME: 30 MINUTES

3 tbsp rapeseed oil
1 tsp cumin seeds
1 tsp coriander seeds
1 Asian bay leaf
4 onions, finely chopped
1 tbsp ground cumin
1 tbsp ground coriander
2 tbsp mixed garlic and ginger paste (see page 7)
1 tsp red chilli powder (more or less to taste)
1 tsp ground turmeric
4 tennis-ball-sized tomatoes, finely chopped
1 tsp salt
100ml (scant 1/2 cup) tomato purée (see page 7) or plain passata (sieved tomatoes)
1.6kg (3lb 8oz) skinless, bone-in chicken thighs
1–2 tsp garam masala

In a large saucepan that has a lid, heat the oil over medium–high heat. When hot, add the cumin seeds, coriander seeds and bay leaf and temper in the oil for about 30 seconds. Pour in the chopped onions. Fry for about 10 minutes until the onions are soft and translucent. Stir in the ground cumin and coriander, garlic and ginger paste, chilli powder and turmeric followed by the chopped tomatoes and allow to sizzle over medium heat for about 5 minutes. Add the salt to this mixture and it will help the onion release moisture into the sauce. The onions and tomatoes will begin to break down, turning into a thick sauce.

Stir in the tomato purée or passata (sieved tomatoes) and sizzle for about 30 seconds, then add the chicken. Stir it all up nicely and pour in just enough water to cover the chicken. Cover the curry and let it simmer for about 10 minutes. The sauce will become nice and thick and will stick to the chicken pieces as they cook.

Remove the lid and stir, adding a drop more water if you prefer a thinner sauce or turn up the heat if it is too runny. You'll know when the curry is ready when the oil comes to the top. Simply skim it off.

Stir in 1 teaspoon of the garam masala and taste. Add more salt if needed. I usually use about 2 teaspoon of garam masala.

MyLahore is a family-run chain that seems to be doing everything right. While researching for this book, I paid them a visit in Bradford and had a lamb curry that was about as close to perfection as they get. The curry I tried was their lamb rogan josh, which I loved, but I was much more interested in the lamb masala curry that was used to make it. The meat was so tender and the flavour was exceptional. I asked the shift manager, Ateeq Bhatti, if I could have the recipe for the meat curry and he was happy to oblige! The recipe I received, however, was to cook about 15 kilos of meat, so it was on an industrial scale as you might expect from a successful restaurant. I've simplified and reduced the recipe for you here.

On page 154 (in the bottom-right corner), I'm cooking up a large batch of lamb masala curry.

LAMB MASALA CURRY

SERVES 8 OR MORE AS PART OF A MULTI-COURSE MEAL

PREP TIME: 10 MINUTES
COOKING TIME: 1 HOUR

200ml (³⁄₄ cup) rapeseed oil
1 bay leaf
5cm (2in) piece of cinnamon
  stick
3 black cardamom pods (or
  6 green pods), bruised
1¹⁄₂ tsp cumin seeds
1¹⁄₂ tsp coriander seeds
2 star anise
3 large onions, finely chopped
4 tbsp mixed garlic and ginger
  paste (see page 7)
4 tomatoes, diced
1 tsp ground turmeric
1¹⁄₂ tbsp bassar curry masala
  (see page 155, optional)
1 tbsp chilli powder
1¹⁄₂ kg (3lb 5oz) lamb leg or
  shoulder, cut into bite-sized
  pieces
2 tbsp plain yoghurt (optional)
Salt

Heat the oil in a large saucepan over medium–high heat. When the oil is visibly hot, add the bay leaf, cinnamon, cardamom pods, cumin and coriander seeds and the star anise and temper the spices in the oil for about 30 seconds. Add the chopped onions and fry for about 5–10 minutes until soft and lightly browned. Stir in the garlic and ginger paste and fry for a further 30 seconds.

Now stir in the tomatoes, turmeric, bassar, if using, and chilli powder. Add the meat and brown for a few minutes, then pour in just enough water to cover. Simmer the lamb for 40 minutes–1 hour until it is good and tender. Don't rush this! If after an hour the meat is not tender enough, cook it longer. The curry is ready when the meat is tender and the oil rises to the top. (I usually skim off the oil.)

To finish, stir in the yoghurt, 1 tablespoon at a time. It will hardly be noticeably in the sauce but thickens and adds flavour to it. Check for seasoning and add salt to taste, then serve.

NOTE: If you can't find bassar, you might want to add a little more chilli powder, but I suggest adding it at the end of cooking to taste. Bassar curry masala contains mustard oil and should always be cooked before trying.

Channa gosht is a favourite staff curry behind the scenes at many restaurants. One of the best I've tried was at Lahore Kebab House in Shoreditch when I was researching recipes for my first book. I didn't get the recipe from them at the time but wished that I had.

This recipe came about by surprise. I was preparing shami kebabs, which are made with the same ingredients. It wasn't untill tried the reduced mixture I was cooking, before blending it all up for the shamis, that I realized that the flavour was so close to that curry I enjoyed so much at Lahore!

I make this curry all the time now. In the recipe, you pan fry the lamb chops, which works well. I also like this curry with grilled (broiled) lamb chops, cooked over hot coals on the barbecue. It adds an amazing smoky, charred flavour.

CHANNA GOSHT

SERVES 4 OR MORE AS PART OF A MULTI-COURSE MEAL

PREP TIME: 20 MINUTES, PLUS MARINATING
COOKING TIME: 1¼ HOURS

3 tbsp ground coriander
2 tbsp ground cumin
1 tsp ground black pepper
1 tsp red chilli powder
1 tsp ground turmeric
1 tbsp paprika
5 tbsp rapeseed oil
1kg (2lb 2oz) lamb chops on the bone
2 large onions, finely chopped
4 green chillies, finely chopped
3 tbsp mixed garlic and ginger paste (see page 7)
400g (14oz) can chopped tomatoes, or chopped fresh tomatoes
150g (scant 1 cup) channa dhal lentils (see page 155), soaked for 20 minutes
Salt
1 tsp garam masala, to sprinkle
3 tbsp chopped coriander (cilantro), to garnish

Stir all of the ground spices together. Mix 1 tablespoon of the oil with 1 heaped tablespoon of the ground spice mixture and rub this into the meat. For best results, let the meat marinate in the spices for 2 hours. When ready to cook, heat 2 tablespoons of oil in a large frying pan over medium–high heat and brown the meat for a couple of minutes on each side. You may need to do this in batches.

Transfer the meat to a plate and pour the rest of the oil into the pan. Fry the onions and chillies over medium–high heat until the onions are soft and translucent. Now add the garlic and ginger paste and the rest of the ground spices. Stir this all up and add the meat, tomatoes, channa dhal and just enough water to cover.

Simmer the curry until the channa dhal is soft and the meat is super tender. This will take about an hour. You may need to add a little water during the cooking process. This is normally a dryer curry, so when your lentils are soft, continue to simmer until you have a thick sauce. Add salt to taste and sprinkle with the garam masala.

Serve garnished with the fresh coriander (cilantro).

WARNING: Watch those lentils! They have a tendency to stick to the pan, so add a little more water and stir occasionally when necessary.

Biryanis can be quite extravagant dishes. Here I have taken a lot of the work out but the flavour is still amazing. Use shop-bought fried onions to make this recipe even easier.

SPECIAL CHICKEN BIRYANI
SERVES 4 OR MORE AS PART OF A MULTI-COURSE MEAL

PREP TIME: 20 MINUTES
COOKING TIME: 40 MINUTES

FOR THE CHICKEN
750g (1lb 10oz) chicken thighs, skinned
2 tbsp mixed garlic and ginger paste (see page 7)
½ tsp ground turmeric
1 tbsp chilli powder (or more or less to taste)
400g (14oz) canned chopped tomatoes or chopped fresh tomatoes
250g (1 cup) plain yoghurt
4 tbsp ghee or rapeseed oil
4 green cardamom pods, bruised
4 cloves
2.5cm (1in) cinnamon stick
1 Asian bay leaf
4 large handfuls of fried onions
A pinch of saffron, infused with 3 tbsp of warm milk
A small bunch of chopped mint leaves, plus extra to serve
A small bunch of chopped coriander (cilantro) leaves, plus extra to serve
Salt

FOR THE RICE
3 tbsp ghee or butter
2 green cardamom pods
1 black cardamom pods
4 cloves
2.5cm (1in) cinnamon stick
8 black peppercorns
1 bay leaf
330g (scant 2 cups) basmati rice, soaked in water for 30 minutes and drained

Cover the chicken with the garlic and ginger paste, turmeric, chilli powder, chopped tomatoes and yoghurt. Really mix well so that the chicken thighs are evenly coated. Set aside to marinate for at least 30 minutes.

Heat the 4 tablespoons ghee or oil in a large saucepan until visibly hot, then add the whole spices. Let the spices sizzle in the oil for about 1 minute. If you don't like biting into whole spices, be sure to count them in and count them back out again. For ease, this can be done after the oil has been seasoned, but I usually leave them in.

Add three-quarters of the fried onions to the spiced oil and set aside. This delicious mixture will be layered into the biryani.

Put the marinated chicken mixture into a large saucepan with the remaining one-quarter of the onions and give it a good stir. Pour in 250ml (1 cup) water, cover and simmer over medium heat for about 10 minutes.

Meanwhile, prepare your rice. Bring 2 litres (8½ cups) lightly salted water to the boil and add the ghee, cardamom pods, cloves, cinnamon stick, peppercorns and bay leaf. Add your soaked rice to the boiling water and cook for about 6 minutes. The rice should be almost cooked, but still with a little bite to it. Strain and set aside.

Returning to your chicken, lift the lid. When the chicken is just cooked through, check for seasoning and add salt to taste. Turn off the heat and carefully layer half of the rice on top of the chicken. Sprinkle with a little saffron milk and half each of the spiced, fried onion mixture, mint leaves and coriander (cilantro) leaves. Cover this layer with the rest of the rice and drizzle the remaining saffron milk, spiced fried onions, coriander and mint over the top. Cover with the lid. Cook over high heat for exactly 8 minutes, then turn the heat off but do not remove the lid for 2 minutes.

To serve, spoon the biryani carefully onto a warmed serving platter. Garnish with a little more mint and coriander, if you like. This delicious biryani is even better topped generously with spicy coriander raita (see page 139).

A few years ago, I was invited to a restaurant called Restaurant 1875 in Ilkley, near Leeds. I believe the restaurant has moved on to Bradford and is now a wine bar, street food and events venue, but back then it was a quaint, authentic and hugely popular Indian restaurant, nestled over the old train station. The head chef, Vivek Kashiwale, showed me this recipe. He had trained under Vineet Bhatia and is now head chef at Mint Leaf of London in Dubai so I feel pretty lucky to have learned this delicious and authentic Goan pork vindaloo from him that day. I have simplified Vivek's recipe for you here but the results are still out of this world.

AUTHENTIC GOAN PORK VINDALOO
SERVES 4 OR MORE AS PART OF A MULTI-COURSE MEAL

PREP TIME: 20 MINUTES, PLUS MARINATING
COOKING TIME: 1½ HOURS

800g (1lb 12oz) pork leg, diced
3–4 tbsp coconut or rapeseed oil
1 head of garlic, cloves cut into thin slivers★
1 tsp brown mustard seeds
10 fresh curry leaves (see page 155)
2 onions, finely chopped
2 tomatoes, finely chopped
1 tsp chilli powder
2 bay leaves
Salt
A squeeze of lemon, to serve

FOR THE MARINADE
1 tsp chilli powder
1½ tbsp ground cumin
1½ tbsp ground coriander
½ tsp ground fenugreek
½ tsp ground cloves
1 tbsp ground black pepper
½ tsp ground turmeric
¾ tsp ground cinnamon
½ tsp ground cardamom
4 green chillies, finely chopped
5 tbsp red wine vinegar
2 tbsp soft brown sugar
1 tbsp tamarind concentrate (or another 2 tbsp of vinegar)
3 tbsp mixed garlic and ginger paste (see page 7)

Start with the marinade. Place all the marinade ingredients in a large glass bowl and stir into a smooth paste. Add the pork and mix well to combine. Cover and leave the pork to marinate in the fridge for 30 minutes or overnight.

When ready to cook, heat the oil in a saucepan over low heat. Add the garlic slivers and allow to cook gently for about 20 minutes. It is important not to burn the garlic, so watch carefully. The garlic should be soft and translucent but not browned. Transfer the garlic from the saucepan to a plate and set aside, leaving as much of the oil in the pan as possible.

Turn up the heat to high and add a little more oil, if required. When visibly hot, stir in the mustard seeds. When they begin to pop, add the curry leaves and sauté for 30 seconds before adding the chopped onions. Reduce the heat to medium–high and fry for about 10 minutes until the onions are soft and translucent.

Add the chopped tomatoes, chilli powder, bay leaves and the pork with all its marinade to the pan, then pour in just enough water to cover. Leave to simmer for about 1 hour, or until the pork is very tender. You may need to add a drop more water while simmering.

To finish, stir in the slivered garlic you sautéed earlier. Check for seasoning and add salt to taste. Squeeze the lemon juice over the top and serve.

★ If you don't want to finely slice all that garlic, you could substitute a large handful of dried garlic flakes. Just simmer them in the sauce until tender.

Staff meals are often the most tasty and different dishes found at Indian restaurants. They usually aren't on the menu and are quite simple, no-fuss meals. Many are family recipes that have been handed down from generation to generation.

This is a dish that I have tried many times and in many different restaurants. It's a Bangladeshi recipe using hilsha fish, which could almost be called the national fish of Bangladesh it's loved so much. I like it but be warned, it is quite difficult to eat as traditionally it is cooked whole and there are lots of small, annoying bones. Hilsha is available in the freezer section at many Asian grocers and online suppliers. The nearest UK-caught fish to hilsha is mackerel or tilapia, both of which are a lot easier to eat!

HILSHA FISH ≡ CURRY SAUCE
SERVES 4 OR MORE AS PART OF A MULTI-COURSE MEAL

PREP TIME: 10 MINUTES
COOKING TIME: 15 MINUTES

FOR THE SAUCE
3 tbsp mustard or rapeseed oil
3 large red onions, thinly sliced
1¹/₂ tbsp garlic paste
2 bird's eye chillies, finely
    chopped
1 tsp ground cumin
1 tsp ground coriander
1 tsp ground turmeric
5 large plum tomatoes, diced,
    or a 400g (14oz) can chopped
    tomatoes
2 tsp garam masala
Juice of 1 lemon
Salt
Chopped coriander (cilantro),
    to serve

FOR THE FISH
4 whole hilsha, mackerel or
    tilapia
2 tbsp rapeseed oil
¹/₂ tsp ground cumin
¹/₂ tsp ground coriander
¹/₂ tsp ground turmeric
Juice of 1 lemon

First make the sauce. Heat the oil in a frying pan over medium–high heat and add the sliced onions. When the onions turn translucent and soft, stir in the garlic paste and bird's eye chillies and fry for about 30 seconds. Spoon in the cumin, coriander and turmeric and fry for 30 seconds, then add the chopped tomatoes. The sauce is quite dry so reduce the tomatoes down to bhuna consistency. If you aren't familiar with bhuna consistency, a nice thick sauce will do. Season with salt to taste and sprinkle in the garam masala. Squeeze in the lemon juice and keep warm while you fry the fish.

Make three shallow slits on each side of the fish and then rub the ground spices and some salt equally over them. Heat another frying pan over medium–high heat and sear the fish for about 2 minutes per side, or until just cooked through. Squeeze the lemon juice over the top.

Serve each fish on a heated plate with the curry sauce and sprinkled with the coriander (cilantro). I like to serve this dish with chickpea, cucumber and tomato salad (see page 148).

If you ever find yourself in the Northern Quarter of Manchester, you'll find some fantastic home-style curry cafés that you've simply got to try. These are no-nonsense restaurants and/or takeaways that look like old greasy spoons but are immaculate and the food is out of this world. You can still get a curry and rice for a fiver! One of my favourites is Al-Faisal Tandoori.

I first visited Al-Faisal Tandoori back in 1998 and little has changed. They still have the green tables with chairs that are attached and water and glasses are on every table. They are only open until 8pm and there is no alcohol on the menu but it is the perfect place for a lunch or early dinner. The food is cooked fresh daily. This simple recipe was given to me on the day I visited by Tariq Malik. I love it!

CHANNA

SERVES 4 OR MORE AS PART OF A MULTI-COURSE MEAL

PREP TIME: 10 MINUTES
COOKING TIME: 1¼ HOURS

4 tbsp rapeseed oil
2 tbsp mixed garlic and ginger paste (see page 7)
250g (1½ cups) dried chickpeas, soaked in water overnight, then drained
½ tsp bicarbonate of soda (baking soda)
1 heaped tbsp cumin seeds
½ tsp ajwain seeds
½ tsp chilli powder
1 onion, finely chopped
Salt
Chopped green chillies and coriander (cilantro), to serve

Heat 1 tablespoon of the oil in a saucepan over medium–high heat until visibly hot. Stir in the garlic and ginger paste and fry for about 1 minute. Now add the prepared chickpeas and bicarbonate of soda and cover with water. Simmer for about 70 minutes, adding a little more water when necessary, until the chickpeas are tender. This is quite a thick curry, so keep the water to a minimum when the chickpeas are close to fork tender.

In a separate frying pan, heat the remaining oil over medium–high heat and temper the cumin seeds and ajwain in the oil for about 40 seconds. Add the chilli powder and chopped onion and fry until the onion is lightly browned and soft. Pour this over your finished chickpeas and give it all a good stir.

Season with salt to taste and serve with chopped green chillies and coriander (cilantro), which can be added to taste at the table.

MAKE THIS CURRY EVEN EASIER: I prefer the texture of slowly simmered dried chickpeas which is how this is made at Al-Faisal Tandoori. I have, however made this recipe using two 400g (14oz) tins of chickpeas with excellent results.

If you like duck, you've simply got to try this authentic Bangladeshi duck curry! The first time I tried it, the duck breasts were marinated in a well-known commercial brand of Balti masala. It was really good but I prefer the simple marinade below. These ingredients really bring out the flavour of the duck without competing with it.

DUCK HAAS PATHA KOBI
SERVES 4 OR MORE AS PART OF A MULTI-COURSE MEAL

PREP TIME: 10 MINUTES
COOKING TIME: 20 MINUTES

4 duck breasts
1 tbsp vegetable oil
1 tbsp garam masala or tandoori
    masala
A pinch of chilli powder
2 tbsp mixed garlic and ginger
    paste (see page 7)
Spring onions (scallions),
    chopped, to serve

FOR THE CABBAGE

3 tbsp vegetable oil
1 tbsp panch phoran
2 tbsp garlic slivers
1 tbsp mixed garlic and ginger
    paste (see page 7)
1 heaped tsp dried chilli (hot
    pepper) flakes (or to taste)
200ml (scant 1 cup) plain
    passata (sieved tomatoes) or
    blended chopped tomatoes
1/2 Savoy cabbage, shredded
Salt

**FOR THE WHOLE
GARAM MASALA**

2 star anise
10 black peppercorns
1 tsp cumin seeds
1 tsp coriander seeds
2.5cm (1in) cinnamon stick

Prepare the duck breast by removing the skin and rubbing the flesh with the oil, garam masala or tandoori masala, chilli powder and the garlic and ginger paste. Set aside to marinate while you prepare the rest of the dish.

Cut each duck skin into 3 pieces and place in a saucepan with 250ml (1 cup) water and all of the whole garam masala ingredients. Simmer the water until reduced to about 5 tablespoons, then strain and put the reduction to one side.

Heat the 3 tablespoons of oil in a saucepan over medium–high heat. Add the panch phoran and fry for about 30 seconds. Now add the garlic slivers and a little salt and fry until the garlic turns light brown. Be careful not to burn the garlic. Stir in the garlic and ginger paste, chilli (hot pepper) flakes and the tomato passata (sieved tomatoes), followed by the shredded cabbage. You just want to just cook the cabbage through so that it still has a bit of crunch to it. Add the duck skin reduction prepared earlier and stir it all up well. Keep warm.

Meanwhile, sear the duck breasts in a dry frying pan over high heat. I prefer my duck slightly pink inside so I cook the breasts for about 2 minutes per side. You can cook for longer if you prefer the meat cooked through.

To serve, slice the duck breasts thinly. Divide the cabbage mixture onto four plates and top each plate with one thinly sliced duck breast. Season with salt to taste and sprinkle with the chopped spring onions (scallions) to serve.

CLASSIC BRITISH CURRIES

When most people think of BIR (British Indian restaurant) style cooking, they picture classic curries such as chicken tikka masala, pathia, Madras and phaal, which were all developed here in the UK. They think of curries like vindaloo, korma and bhuna, which share names with dishes that originated in the Indian subcontinent but bear little resemblance to their namesakes. These curries and many others became hugely popular in Britain because they were developed to please the palate of the general public. They may differ in heat level and flavour but they all have several things in common: meat is served off the bone; they are all made with a prepared base curry sauce; and are all therefore cheap, quick and easy to prepare.

If you have a copy of my first book, *The Curry Guy*, you may know that cooking curries the BIR way takes some forward preparation. Over the past year I have worked on developing ways that you can make authentic BIR-style curries without the need for all the forward preparation done at restaurants. This forward preparation is done to speed up the cooking process and also for flavour. Following are a few things you can do to cut corners while still making a curry that will rank right up there with those served at the best curry houses.

THE BASE CURRY SAUCE

I have included two base sauces in this book. On page 51, you will find one that is similar to many I have seen made at restaurants. On page 50 you will find my cheat's method, which is much quicker. When onions are slowly stewed in oil and water, they become sweeter and develop a flavour that is recognized worldwide in British curries. My cheat's method may not have the same sweetness but it's a lot faster and close enough to get excellent results!

PRE-COOKED MEATS, POULTRY AND VEGETABLES

When recipes call for pre-cooked meat, poultry or potatoes, this is done for speed. It's how it is done at curry houses. Of course you can add these ingredients to the different sauces raw. Just ensure you top with enough water or stock to simmer until the meat/vegetables are cooked through and tender. This will take more time but will turn out delicious all the same.

MIXED POWDER

Mixed powder is one of the curry house secrets that will take your BIR curries to the next level. It is essentially a fancy curry powder. If mixing the ingredients sounds too much like hard work, use a good-quality curry powder instead. This recipe makes 17 tablespoons or enough for about eight curries that serve four.

3 tbsp cumin powder
3 tbsp ground coriander
3 tbsp paprika
3 tbsp turmeric
4 tbsp curry powder
1 tbsp garam masala

One of the questions I get asked most often is whether or not you have to make a BIR base curry sauce to achieve that famous curry house flavour. The answer is 'yes', but you can cheat a bit. I would like to stress that a base curry sauce is essentially an authentic Indian base masala sauce, like those featured in countless Indian cookbooks, that has been developed at restaurants across the UK for speed, ease and economy. It is the liquid needed to cook the curry.

This recipe makes enough base curry sauce for two to three curries that serve four people. This is a quick substitute for the large batch. It doesn't include as many ingredients but still works exceptionally well.

QUICK ᴬᴺᴰ EASY
BASE CURRY SAUCE (CHEAT'S METHOD)
MAKES ABOUT 1.5 LITRES/6 CUPS (7–8 PORTIONS)

PREP TIME: 10 MINUTES
COOKING TIME: 20 MINUTES

2 tbsp rapeseed oil or melted ghee
3 brown onions (about 600g/1lb 5oz), finely chopped
1/4 red pepper (bell pepper), diced
1 tbsp mixed garlic and ginger paste (see page 7)
1 large tomato, diced
1/2 tsp ground cumin
1/2 tsp ground coriander
1/2 tsp paprika
1/4 tsp ground turmeric
1/4 tsp ground fenugreek
1 litre (4 cups) water, for thinning

Heat the oil over medium–high heat in a medium saucepan. When hot, toss in the chopped onions and red pepper (bell pepper) and sauté for about 5 minutes until the onion is soft and translucent but not browned. Add all the remaining ingredients except the water or stock, and stir it all up well. Fry for a further 30 seconds or so, then add 250ml (1 cup) water. Turn up the heat and simmer for 5–10 minutes until the water has evaporated by half and your veggies are nice and soft.

Add another 250ml (1 cup) water and blend this mixture – either with a hand-held blender or countertop blender – until very smooth. Depending on the blender you use, this can take a couple of minutes. Once smooth, add another 500ml (2 cups) water. The sauce should be about the same consistency as full-fat milk, so add more water if needed.

TIP: I often substitute some of the cooking stock from the chicken masala curry (see page 34) or lamb masala curry (see page 35) for the water, depending on the type of curry I am making. You can easily double up this recipe if you'd like to make more.

Base curry sauces vary from restaurant to restaurant so there is no one recipe. The most important thing to understand is that it is essentially a smooth onion stock with small amounts of other vegetables and spices thrown in. It is bland, but it has to be as it is only a base liquid that is added to many different curries from mild to spicy.

As long as you end up with a sauce that is about the same consistency as full fat milk, you're ready to start cooking! This sauce keeps in the fridge for up to three days in air-tight containers and can be frozen for up to three months.

BASE CURRY SAUCE
MAKES ABOUT 3 LITRES/13 CUPS (14–16 PORTIONS)

PREP TIME: 20 MINUTES
COOKING TIME: 50 MINUTES

1kg (about 6 medium) brown (Spanish) onions, roughly chopped
350ml (1½ cups) rapeseed oil
¼ red (bell) pepper
4 tbsp mixed garlic and ginger paste (see page 7)
150g (5½oz) canned chopped tomatoes or chopped fresh tomatoes
30g (1oz) cabbage, shredded
30g (1oz) carrot, chopped
2 tsp ground cumin
2 tsp ground coriander
2 tsp ground turmeric
2 tsp paprika
2 tsp ground fenugreek
2 tsp garam masala

Put the chopped onions in a large saucepan that has a lid. Then add the rest of the ingredients, including the oil, and 1 litre (4 cups) water. Bring to a rolling simmer over medium–high heat, then reduce the heat to medium and cover. Allow to simmer for about 45 minutes, stirring occasionally.

After 45 minutes most of the oil will have risen to the top. Turn off the heat and skim as much off as you can. (This is seasoned oil – it can be used to cook your curries instead of plain oil. It keeps in an airtight container indefinitely, though my seasoned oil is rarely around long.)

Blend the stock for about 2–4 minutes until very smooth. It is easiest to use a hand-held blender if you have one, but you could do this in batches in a countertop blender. Once blended and smooth, you will have a very thick sauce. If not using immediately, I recommend placing this in the fridge or freezer to save space. If using immediately, add water until the sauce is the same consistency as full-fat milk – about another 1 litre (4 cups) should do.

TIP: I usually freeze the sauce before diluting in 500–750ml (2–3 cup) portions to save freezer space. Then I dilute the defrosted sauce with water or stock until it is the same consistency as full-fat milk for use in my curries.

(GF) (BIR)

If you like prawn (shrimp) curries, this is a straightforward one that my 14-year- old daughter, Jennifer, makes all the time. One of her tips for getting extra flavour into the curry (that isn't in the recipe method below) is to purchase your prawns unpeeled. Peel and clean them and then sauté the shells in the oil. The shells will turn pink as they cook. Press the shells down to extract every last bit of flavour and then remove and discard them leaving, as much oil in the pan as possible. Then, start the recipe as described below. This extra step really adds depth and flavour to the sauce.

PRAWN MASALA CURRY
SERVES 4 OR MORE AS PART OF A MULTI-COURSE MEAL

PREP TIME: 10 MINUTES, PLUS MAKING THE BASE CURRY SAUCE
COOKING TIME: 10 MINUTES

3 tbsp rapeseed oil or ghee
1 tsp mustard seeds
2.5cm (1in) cinnamon stick
10 curry leaves (see page 155) (optional)
2 tbsp mixed garlic and ginger paste (see page 7)
2 green chillies, finely chopped
2 tbsp mixed powder (see page 49) or curry powder
50ml (3½ tbsp) tomato purée (see page 7)
400ml (1¾ cups) base curry sauce (see pages 50 or 51)
600g (1lb 5oz) raw bite-sized prawns (shrimp), peeled and cleaned
200ml (scant 1 cup) thick coconut milk
2 tbsp light soy sauce or coconut amino (see page 155)
1 small bunch of coriander (cilantro), finely chopped
Salt and freshly ground black pepper
Juice of 1–2 limes
1 tsp garam masala

Heat the oil in a large frying pan. When visibly hot, toss in the mustard seeds and cinnamon stick. The mustard seeds will begin to pop. When they do, add the curry leaves and fry for about 15 seconds until they become fragrant.

Stir in the garlic and ginger paste and bring to a good sizzle before adding the chopped chillies. Stir it all up well, then add the mixed powder, tomato purée and about 125ml (½ cup) of the base curry sauce. Allow this to come to a simmer, only stirring if the sauce is catching on the pan. If the sauce caramelizes to the sides of the pan, stir it in as it adds nice flavour.

Tip in the raw prawns (shrimp) and the rest of the base curry sauce and simmer until the prawns are cooked through and you are happy with the consistency of the sauce. Now add the coconut milk and the soy sauce or coconut amino. Stir in the chopped coriander (cilantro) and season with salt and pepper to taste.

To serve, squeeze the lime juice over the top and sprinkle with the garam masala.

NOTE: Most soy sauces are not gluten free. If this is important to you, use coconut amino.

My friend Richard Sayce (AKA Misty Ricardo) records popular YouTube videos demonstrating his take on British Indian Restaurant cooking and he sent me this recipe to try. This is my interpretation of it. It's spicy and sweet. Kids love it too, but you might want to omit or reduce the amount of fresh chillies and chilli powder. Richard adds large chunks of fresh mango to this curry, but I opted for small chunks. It's a personal thing, so do what you think will taste best.

MANGO CHICKEN CURRY
SERVES 4 OR MORE AS PART OF A MULTI-COURSE MEAL

PREP TIME: 10 MINUTES, PLUS MAKING THE BASE CURRY SAUCE
COOKING TIME: 15 MINUTES

2 tbsp rapeseed oil
2 tbsp mixed garlic and ginger paste (see page 7)
1 tbsp mixed powder (see page 49) or curry powder
1 tsp chilli powder (or to taste)
3 tbsp finely chopped coriander (cilantro) stalks
2 fresh green chillies (bird's eye or bullet), thinly sliced
600ml (2½ cups) base curry sauce (see pages 50 or 51), heated (plus more if required)
6 tbsp coconut flour
4 tbsp smooth mango chutney
700g (1lb 9oz) pre-cooked chicken (see page 34)
1 small mango, cut into bite-sized chunks (canned mango can be used)
1 tsp garam masala
1 tsp dried methi leaves
Salt
3 tbsp finely chopped coriander (cilantro) leaves, to serve

Heat the oil in a frying pan over medium–high heat. When visibly hot, stir in the garlic and ginger paste and let it fry for about 30 seconds. Stir in the mixed powder and chilli powder, along with the finely chopped coriander (cilantro) stalks and fresh chillies. Stir these ingredients really well into the hot oil, then add about 250ml (1 cup) of the base curry sauce.

Let this come to a rolling simmer, stirring only if it is sticking to the pan. Add the coconut flour and mango chutney, followed by another 125ml (½ cup) of base curry sauce. Stir in the chicken and heat it through for about 1 minute in the bubbling sauce. Now add the mango chunks and the rest of the base curry sauce. Let the curry cook for another 4 minutes or so until it has reduced down to your preferred consistency. You can always add more base sauce or a little water if it becomes too dry.

To finish, season with salt to taste and sprinkle the garam masala and dried methi leaves over the top. Give it a good stir and garnish with the fresh coriander (cilantro) leaves to serve.

Fresh fenugreek leaves are surprisingly still difficult to come by at most supermarkets. You will almost definitely find them at Asian grocers. Last year I tried to grow some of my own and the plants actually thrived! I kill everything I plant, but for some reason my fenugreek just took off. So if you enjoy growing your own herbs, give it a try.

CHICKEN METHI CURRY
SERVES 4 OR MORE AS PART OF A MULTI-COURSE MEAL

PREP TIME: 10 MINUTES, PLUS SOAKING AND MAKING THE BASE CURRY SAUCE
COOKING TIME: 10 MINUTES

½ tsp salt
1 large handful of fresh fenugreek (methi) leaves*, roughly chopped
3 tbsp rapeseed oil
2 star anise
1 Asian bay leaf
1 tsp coriander seeds
1 tsp fennel seeds
1 onion, finely chopped
2 tbsp mixed garlic and ginger paste (see page 7)
2 green chilies, finely chopped
Stalks from a large bunch of coriander (cilantro)
1 tbsp mixed powder (see page 49) or curry powder
1 tsp bassar curry masala (see page 155) or chilli powder
75ml (5 tbsp) plain passata (sieved tomatoes) or blended chopped tomatoes
500ml (2 cups) base curry sauce (see pages 50 or 51), heated
700g (1lb 9oz) pre-cooked chicken (see page 34), plus 120ml (½ cup) of the cooking stock
4 tbsp plain yoghurt
Salt
3 tbsp chopped coriander (cilantro) leaves
½ tsp garam masala
1 tsp dried methi leaves

* See page 7 for fresh fenugreek substitutes

Fresh fenugreek has a tendency to be very bitter. To reduce the bitterness, pour the ½ teaspoon salt over the leaves and mix thoroughly by hand. Set aside for 10 minutes. After 10 minutes, squeeze the leaves to get rid of any excess water, which will also get rid of the bitterness. Finely chop the leaves.

Now heat the rapeseed oil in a large pan over medium–high heat. When visibly hot, stir in the star anise, bay leaf, coriander seeds and fennel seeds and temper them in the oil for about 40 seconds. Add the finely chopped onion and fry for about 2 minutes, followed by the garlic and ginger paste. Stir this all up well, then add the green chillies, coriander (cilantro) stalks, fenugreek leaves, mixed powder and bassar curry masala or chilli powder.

Fry for a further 30 seconds, then add the passata (sieved tomatoes), 250ml (1 cup) of the base curry sauce and the cooked chicken. Move the pieces of chicken around in the sauce to coat them but only stir the sauce if it is obviously sticking to the pan. Add the remaining base sauce and bring to a rapid simmer. Cook until the sauce is your preferred consistency, then whisk in the plain yoghurt, 1 tablespoon at a time. Season with salt to taste and garnish with the freshly chopped coriander, garam masala and dried methi.

(GF) (BIR)

Shimla mirch means bell pepper or capsicum and you get a lot of that in this one. You could try making this curry with tandoori chicken tikka but I prefer it with chicken keema. Both are really good. At restaurants, this popular keema curry is usually prepared with minced (ground) lamb. You could use your minced meat of choice. Turkey is nice too. The curry is often topped with julienned ginger, spring onions (scallions), coriander (cilantro) and freshly chopped green chillies and that is exactly what you'll be doing here. The toppings take a good curry and make it great!

CHICKEN KEEMA SHIMLA MIRCH
SERVES 4 OR MORE AS PART OF A MULTI-COURSE MEAL

**PREP TIME: 15 MINUTES,
PLUS MAKING THE BASE
CURRY SAUCE
COOKING TIME: 15 MINUTES**

3 tbsp rapeseed oil
1 onion, roughly chopped
2 large green (bell) pepper,
   roughly chopped
1–2 green chillies, finely
   chopped, plus extra sliced
   chillies to serve
2 tbsp mixed garlic and ginger
   paste (see page 7)
1–2 tbsp Madras curry powder
1 tsp ground cumin
1 tsp round coriander
1 tsp red chilli powder
1/2 tsp ground turmeric
3 tbsp plain passata (sieved
   tomatoes) or blended tomatoes
600ml (2 1/2 cups) base curry sauce
   (see pages 50 or 51), heated
600g (1lb 5oz) minced (ground)
   chicken
200ml (3/4 cup) thick coconut milk
5 small tomatoes, quartered
Salt

TOPPINGS TO SERVE
5cm (2in) piece of peeled ginger,
   julienned
4 spring onions (scallions),
   roughly chopped
5 tbsp finely chopped coriander
   (cilantro)

Heat the oil over medium–high heat. When it's visibly hot, add the chopped onion, green (bell) peppers and green chillies and fry until the onion is translucent but still quite crisp. Add the garlic and ginger paste and stir it all in for about 1 minute.

Now add the ground spices and stir them into the vegetables. Pour in the tomato passata (sieved tomatoes) and 250ml (1 cup) of the curry sauce. Bring this to a simmer, stirring only if the sauce is sticking to the pan.

Add the chicken and stir it into the sauce. Let this simmer for about 10 minutes until the chicken is cooked through. (In restaurants, pre-cooked keema would be used as a time saver so if you're working ahead, feel free to do the same.) Once cooked through, add the rest of the base sauce and the coconut milk and stir it all to combine.

Add the quartered tomatoes. Season with salt to taste and add more of the ground spices, if you want. Serve at the table with the ginger, spring onions (scallions), coriander (cilantro) and sliced chillies on the side or as a garnish. I have provided quantities for the toppings to start, but you might just find you like them so much you want to add more.

In order to make a traditional Birmingham Balti, it must be made and served in an authentic Balti pan. In Balti kitchens, the curries are cooked over intensely high heat. Often the curry catches fire but it doesn't burn. The fire is just the oil being burnt and it gives a nice smoky, charred flavour to the curry. For the home chef, go ahead and use a pan you're comfortable using and turn the heat right up. It won't be the 'real deal' but it will still taste amazing!

A good wok, for example will do the job just fine. If you're really into baltis, you might be happy to know that authentic Balti pans like those produced in the 1970s are once again being made in the UK. These are great not only for cooking but serving right from the pan just as baltis are meant to be eaten. See suppliers (page 156) for more information.

LAMB KEEMA SAAG BALTI
SERVES 4 OR MORE AS PART OF A MULTI-COURSE MEAL

PREP TIME: 10 MINUTES
COOKING TIME: 15 MINUTES

3 tbsp rapeseed oil or ghee
1 tsp panch poran (see page 155)
2 onions, finely chopped or thinly sliced
2 tbsp mixed garlic and ginger paste (see page 7)
2 red or green chillies, finely chopped
2 tbsp curry powder
500g (1lb 2 oz) minced (ground) lamb
150ml (²/₃ cup) plain passata (sieved tomatoes) or blended chopped tomatoes
150g (5¹/₂oz) baby spinach leaves, washed and shredded
Up to 250ml (1 cup) base curry sauce (see pages 50 or 51), heated (optional)
Salt
1 tsp garam masala, to serve

Heat the oil over medium heat. When visibly hot, toss in the panch poran and temper the spices for about 30 seconds, then add the onions. Sauté for about 5 minutes until soft and translucent.

Add the garlic and ginger paste and the chopped chillies. Fry for a further 1 minute, then stir in the curry powder followed by the lamb. Brown the meat for a couple of minutes and stir in the passata (sieved tomatoes) and shredded spinach. The spinach will wilt and cook into the sauce.

To finish, stir in the base curry sauce if you prefer a saucier curry. Let it simmer until it cooks down to your preferred consistency. Season with salt to taste and sprinkle with garam masala to serve. Baltis are dry curries, perfect for mopping up with hot naans.

Aloo gosht, or potatoes with meat, makes an excellent meal on its own. I do usually serve it with rice, chapattis and/or naans, but there are plenty of carbs in the potatoes. You could simply serve it on its own as you would a stew. The bassar curry masala mentioned in this recipe is used mainly in Pakistani cuisine. It is spicy like chilli powder but has other ingredients thrown in, including mustard oil powder. It should be cooked before it is eaten and adds a really nice flavour.

ALOO GOSHT

SERVES 4 OR MORE AS PART OF A MULTI-COURSE MEAL

PREP TIME: 10 MINUTES, PLUS MAKING THE BASE CURRY SAUCE, COOKING THE POTATOES AND MEAT
COOKING TIME: 15 MINUTES

5 tbsp rapeseed, vegetable oil or ghee
1 tsp cumin seeds
1 onion, finely chopped
2 tbsp mixed garlic and ginger paste (see page 7)
1 tsp red chilli (hot pepper) flakes
1 tsp bassar curry masala or chilli powder (or to taste)
1 tsp paprika
1/2 tsp ground turmeric
2 tsp ground cumin
1 tsp ground coriander
500ml (2 cups) base curry sauce (see pages 50 or 51), heated
125ml (1/2 cup) plain passata (sieved tomatoes) or blended chopped tomatoes
750g (1lb 10oz) pre-cooked lamb or the meat from lamb masala curry (see page 35), plus 150ml (2/3 cup) stock from the lamb masala curry (or more base curry sauce)
450g (1lb) cooked potatoes, peeled and diced
Salt
1 tsp garam masala
3 tbsp finely chopped coriander (cilantro) leaves

Heat the oil in a large saucepan over medium–high heat. When visibly hot, add the cumin seeds and temper in the oil for about 30 seconds. Add the chopped onion and fry until soft and translucent – about 5 minutes should do the job. (This is a curry that benefits from cooking the chopped onion longer until browned so you can do that if you have time.)

Stir in the garlic and ginger paste and allow to sizzle for about 30 seconds, then add the chilli (hot pepper) flakes, bassar curry masala, paprika, turmeric, cumin and ground coriander. Stir this into the onion mixture. It will become quite fragrant after 30 seconds. When this happens, stir in half of the base curry sauce and the passata (sieved tomatoes). Bring to a rolling simmer, only stirring if the sauce is sticking to the pan.

Stir in the lamb pieces and potato chunks with the cooking stock and the rest of the base curry sauce. Heat everything through and reduce the sauce down to your preferred consistency. Season with salt to taste. To serve, sprinkle with the garam masala and chopped coriander (cilantro).

Like many of my recipes, I found this one by chance. I was in Tooting, London, with my wife one evening and we happened upon a restaurant called Vijaya Krishna. We both ordered the Alleppey lamb roast off the menu and absolutely loved it. I asked for the recipe and thankfully the chef Shabaz Ali was happy to invite me back to the kitchen the next day. This is my interpretation of their excellent dish. It is a dry curry and definitely worth a try!

To make it, you need to start with small pieces (tikka) of pre-cooked lamb. I often simmer the lamb tikka in base curry sauce until cooked and tender. The lamb-flavoured base sauce is then delicious used in other lamb curries. Dry the meat before frying. This is a great way to use up leftover lamb roast from Sunday dinner, too. The most important part of getting this dish right is to ensure that, however you cook your lamb, it is good and tender before adding it to the pan. The recipe serves two, but it can easily be scaled up to serve more.

QUICK STIR-FRIED LAMB
SERVES 2 OR MORE AS PART OF A MULTI-COURSE MEAL

PREP TIME: 10 MINUTES
COOKING TIME: 10 MINUTES

3 tbsp rapeseed oil
1 large onion, finely chopped
2 green chillies, finely chopped
20 fresh or frozen curry leaves
   (see page 155)
1 generous tbsp mixed garlic and
   ginger paste (see page 7)
400–500g (14–18oz) pre-cooked
   lamb (from leg or shoulder)
1 tbsp mixed powder (see
   page 49) or curry powder
$1/2$ tsp chilli powder
1 tbsp freshly ground black
   pepper (or to taste)
1–2 tbsp dark soy sauce
Salt
3 tbsp finely chopped coriander
   (cilantro) leaves
Lemon wedges

Heat the oil in a large frying pan over high heat. When visibly hot, add the chopped onion and fry for about 5 minutes until lightly browned. Stir in the fresh green chillies and the curry leaves and fry for a further 30 seconds until fragrant. Add the garlic and ginger paste and fry for another 30 seconds.

Add the lamb tikka and fry over high heat until heated through and crisp. Stir in the mixed powder, chilli powder, black pepper and soy sauce and season with a little salt, if needed.

To serve, garnish with the chopped coriander (cilantro) and the lemon wedges, which can be squeezed over the top at the table.

In Hindi, achar means pickle. Achari is a very popular Punjabi curry made with the spices often used to make pickles, such as the panch poran and dried chillies used in this recipe. The sweet flavour of the mango chutney and sourness in the lime pickle give this curry the well-rounded flavour loved by so many.

LAMB ACHARI

SERVES 4 OR MORE AS PART OF A MULTI-COURSE MEAL

PREP TIME: 10 MINUTES, PLUS MAKING THE BASE CURRY SAUCE AND COOKING THE LAMB COOKING TIME: 10 MINUTES

4 tbsp rapeseed or vegetable oil
1 tbsp panch poran (see page 155)
2 dried Kashmiri chillies, split lengthwise and deseeded
1 onion, thinly sliced into rings
2 tbsp mixed garlic and ginger paste (see page 7)
2 bird's eye chillies, finely chopped
125ml (½ cup) tomato purée (see page 7), plain passata (sieved tomatoes) or blended canned tomatoes
2 tbsp mixed powder (see page 49) or curry powder
1 tsp ground coriander
1 tsp Kashmiri chilli powder
600ml (2½ cups) base curry sauce (see pages 50 or 51), heated
750g (1lb 10oz) pre-cooked lamb (see page 35), plus 200ml (¾ cup) of the cooking stock
2 tbsp lime pickle (or 1 tbsp each of lime pickle and smooth mango chutney)
4 tbsp plain yoghurt
1 tsp dried fenugreek (methi) leaves
1 tsp garam masala
Juice of 1 lemon
Salt
3 tbsp finely chopped coriander (cilantro) leaves, to serve

Heat the oil in a frying pan over medium–high heat. When the oil is visibly hot, add the panch poran and Kashmiri chillies. The panch poran will begin to crackle as the spices release their flavour into the oil. Toss in the sliced onion and fry until soft and translucent. A sprinkle of salt will help release moisture from the onion and cool down the pan.

Add the garlic and ginger paste and bird's eye chillies and fry for a further 30 seconds while stirring continuously. Pour in the tomato purée followed by the mixed powder, ground coriander, chilli powder and 250ml (1 cup) of the base curry sauce. It will sizzle and bubble, but don't be tempted to stir unless it is obviously burning to the pan. Be sure to scrape any caramelized sauce from the side of the pan into the sauce for additional flavour.

Add the meat and its stock and the rest of the curry sauce and simmer until it has reduced down to your preferred consistency. Stir in the lime pickle and mango chutney, if using, then add the yoghurt 1 tablespoon at a time. You need to stir continuously so that the yoghurt doesn't curdle.

Swirl in the dried fenugreek leaves and garam masala and check for seasoning, adding salt to taste. Squeeze the lemon juice over the top and garnish with the fresh coriander (cilantro) to serve.

FOUR BRITISH CLASSIC CURRY SAUCES IN A HURRY

Most of the preceding BIR recipes were all developed to serve four. Here I would like to show you a few of the most popular BIR curries, cooked as they would be in a curry house. Curry-house portions are made to share, so they usually serve one to two people so that a group of friends can all order their favourite and share some of it around the table.

As these recipes are prepared the curry house way over high heat, it is a good idea to have any required pre-cooked ingredients at the ready so that you can whip these up in minutes.

★ Each of the following makes a standard curry house sized portion and serves 1–2 or more if part of a multi-curry meal.

★ Add anything you like to the following sauces. Raw prawns (shrimp) and chicken should cook through quickly. That said, you might want to use a pre-cooked tandoori or stewed version of each instead. Red meat and potatoes should be pre-cooked so that they are tender when added.

★ If you prepare the spice masalas (blends) for each curry before cooking, it will be much easier to cook without checking the recipe. If you have a favourite curry, you can double or triple the spice masala (blends) and store in an airtight container in a cupboard so that you have more on hand when required.

★ Add 200–250g (7–9oz) of the main ingredient, such as chicken, lamb, paneer (see page 155) or par-cooked vegetables, per person. If you're really hungry, add more!

★ A fun challenge: try reducing the preceding BIR recipes to make these smaller curry-house portions. If you have my first cookbook, you can do the same with those classic recipes.

TIKKA MASALA SAUCE

SERVES 1–2

PREP TIME: 5 MINUTES
COOKING TIME: 15 MINUTES

SPICE MASALA FOR THIS CURRY
(MAKES 7 TBSP)
1¹/₂ tsp sugar
1 tbsp ground almonds
1 tbsp coconut flour
1 tbsp mixed powder (see page 49) or curry powder
1 tbsp tandoori masala
1¹/₂ tsp sweet paprika

FOR THE SAUCE
2 tbsp rapeseed oil or ghee
1 tbsp mixed garlic and ginger paste (see page 7)
3 tbsp tomato purée (see page 7)
350ml (1¹/₂ cups) base curry sauce (see pages 50 or 51), heated
125ml (¹/₂ cup) single (light) cream
1 tsp dried fenugreek (methi) leaves
Lemon juice, to taste
Salt
1 tbsp finely chopped coriander (cilantro) leaves, to garnish
A pinch of garam masala, to sprinkle

Combine all the ingredients for the spice blend.

Heat the oil in a large frying pan over high heat. When visibly hot, stir in the garlic and ginger paste. Let this fry for about 30 seconds, then add all the tikka spice masala and tomato purée and stir it all up. Now add about 125ml (¹/₂ cup) of the base curry sauce and let it come to a simmer for about 1 minute. Only stir if it is catching to the pan.

When the base sauce begins to dry up, add the remaining base sauce and your main ingredient of choice. Simmer to heat the main ingredients through or cook through if raw. Add more base sauce or water if needed to stop the curry from going dry. Reduce the sauce down to your preferred consistency.

To finish, stir in the cream and sprinkle with the methi leaves. Squeeze a little lemon juice over the top and add salt to taste. Garnish with the chopped coriander (cilantro) and garam masala to serve.

KORMA SAUCE

SERVES 1–2

PREP TIME: 5 MINUTES
COOKING TIME: 10 MINUTES

SPICE MASALA FOR THIS CURRY
(MAKES 5 TBSP)
2 green cardamom pods, lightly bruised
1¹/₂ tbsp sugar, or to taste
3 tbsp ground almonds
1 tbsp coconut flour

FOR THE SAUCE
2 tbsp rapeseed oil or ghee
2.5cm (1in) piece of cinnamon stick
2 green cardamom pods, bruised
¹/₂ tbsp mixed garlic and ginger paste (see page 7)
400ml (1³/₄ cups) base curry sauce (see pages 50 or 51), heated
70g (2¹/₂oz) block coconut cream, or 2 extra tbsp coconut flour
60ml (¹/₄ cup) single (light) cream, plus a little more to finish
1 tsp rose water, or to taste
1 tbsp cold butter (optional)
Salt
1 tsp garam masala, to serve

Combine all the ingredients for the spice blend.

Heat the oil in a large frying pan over high heat. When visibly hot, toss in the cinnamon stick and cardamom pods and fry for about 30 seconds. Add the garlic and ginger paste and fry for a further 30 seconds before adding all of the korma spice masala. Stir the masala into the oil and then top with about 250ml (1 cup) of the base curry sauce. Let simmer for about 1 minute, adding more base sauce if it is drying up and only stirring if it is catching to the pan.

Add the rest of the base sauce and the block coconut, breaking it up so that it dissolves into the sauce. Add your main ingredient of choice and simmer until heated through, or cooked through if raw. Stir in the cream, rose water and butter (if using). Season with salt and perhaps a little more sugar to taste. Garnish with a drizzle more cream and a sprinkling of garam masala.

JALFREZI SAUCE

SERVES 1–2

PREP TIME: 5 MINUTES
COOKING TIME: 10 MINUTES

SPICE MASALA FOR THIS CURRY
(MAKES 2 TBSP)
1²/₃ tbsp mixed powder (see page 49) or curry powder
1 tsp chilli powder (or to taste)

FOR THE SAUCE
2 tbsp rapeseed oil
¹/₂ onion, thinly sliced
¹/₂ red pepper (bell pepper), deseeded and thinly sliced
2 green bird's eye chillies, cut into thin rings,
    plus 2 more, split lengthways, to serve
1 tbsp finely chopped coriander (cilantro) stalks
1 tbsp mixed garlic and ginger paste (see page 7)
4 tbsp tomato purée (see page 7)
250ml (1 cup) base curry sauce (see pages 50
    or 51), heated
2 cherry tomatoes, quartered
¹/₂ tsp dried fenugreek (methi) leaves
Salt
¹/₂ tsp garam masala, to sprinkle
Chopped coriander (cilantro) leaves, to garnish

Heat the oil in a large frying pan until visibly hot.
Toss in the sliced onion and pepper (bell pepper)
along with the sliced chillies and fry for a couple
of minutes. The veggies should still be quite
crisp. Stir in the coriander (cilantro) stalks and
the garlic and ginger paste and sauté for another
30 seconds. Stir in all the spice masala and the
tomato purée, mixing well as you do.

Pour in half of the base sauce and let it come to a
rapid simmer for a couple of minutes, stirring only
if it is sticking to the pan. Add a little more base
sauce or a drop of water if it becomes too dry. Add
your main ingredient of choice and heat through,
or cook through if adding raw. Stir in the rest of the
base sauce to help the main ingredients cook
through. You can always add more sauce if needed!

To finish, stir in the cherry tomatoes and dried
methi leaves. Season with salt and sprinkle the
garam masala over the top. Garnish with the fresh
coriander (cilantro) and the split bird's eye chillies.

PHAAL SAUCE

SERVES 1–2

PREP TIME: 10 MINUTES
COOKING TIME: 10 MINUTES

SPICE MASALA FOR THIS CURRY
(MAKES 3 TBSP)
2 tbsp red hot chilli powder
1 tbsp mixed powder (see page 49) or curry powder

FOR THE SAUCE
2 tbsp rapeseed oil or ghee
¹/₂ onion, finely sliced
1 red pepper (bell pepper), finely sliced
5 green bird's eye chillies, cut into thin rings
4 Scotch bonnet chillies, finely chopped
1 tbsp mixed garlic and ginger paste (see page 7)
125ml (¹/₂ cup) tomato purée (see page 7)
250ml (1 cup) base curry sauce (see pages 50
    or 51), heated
1 tbsp Mr Naga chilli pickle★
Salt
Chopped coriander (cilantro) leaves, to garnish
Julienned ginger, to garnish

Heat the oil in a large frying pan until visibly hot.
Add the sliced onion, (bell) pepper and all the
chillies. Fry for a couple of minutes until the
onion turns soft and translucent. Stir in the
garlic and ginger paste and fry for a further
30 seconds. Add the spice masala and sizzle for a
further 30 seconds. Are you feeling the pain yet?

Cool it all down by pouring in the tomato
purée. It will bubble right up. When it does, pour
in 150ml (²/₃ cup) of the base curry sauce. Leave
to simmer for about 2 minutes without stirring
unless it is obviously sticking to the pan. Add
your main ingredient of choice followed by the
rest of the base curry sauce.

Simmer until you have the sauce consistency
you want. To finish, spoon in the Mr Naga pickle
and season with salt. Garnish with chopped
coriander (cilantro) and julienned ginger.

★ Mr Naga pickle can be purchased at Asian
grocers. It's used for fiery hot curries in many
restaurants. It's not only hot, it tastes great too.

SEAFOOD RECIPES

I could literally write a few books of seafood and freshwater fish recipes. I love seafood as there are so many things you can do with it. The thing is, I enjoy a good grilled (broiled) seabream or bass with nothing more than a little salt and pepper and a twist of lemon. Fish doesn't need a lot of additional ingredients to make it amazing.

For this reason, I have found cooking Indian inspired seafood and fish dishes a bit of a challenge over the years. You don't want to overpower the main ingredient, but complement it. The halibut curry on page 77 was one of those challenges that ended up working really well, I think. There may be a lot of ingredients but the meaty halibut can stand up to them. The rest of the recipes in this section are all much simpler. Whether you prefer extravagant or simple fish dishes, I hope you will try each of these recipes.

I have always loved crab dishes. One of my favourites is an Indian dish called butter crab. It is what it says: live crabs thrown into a large pot of boiling ghee (clarified butter) and it's so good. Give it a try sometime. This recipe is a whole lot better for you. The sauce is sweet, sour and just a bit spicy. You could always add more chillies or even chilli powder, but not too much! It will take away from all the lovely flavours going on in this dish.

I suggest purchasing freshly dressed crabs from your fishmonger. It's a lot easier than cooking and cleaning live crabs. Serve this one with plain white rice or French bread.

20-MINUTE COCONUT MASALA CRAB CURRY

SERVES 2–4

PREP TIME: 10 MINUTES
COOKING TIME: 15 MINUTES

2 tbsp rapeseed oil
20 curry leaves (see page 155)
1 tbsp fennel seeds
¼ tsp fenugreek seeds
1 onion, finely chopped
4 shallots, finely chopped
1 tbsp mixed garlic and ginger paste (see page 7)
2 green chillies, finely chopped
1 tsp ground turmeric
1 tsp ground cumin
4 tennis ball-sized tomatoes, finely chopped
400ml (14 fl oz) can thick coconut milk
2 cooked dressed crabs, quartered
1 tsp jaggery or light brown sugar
1 tbsp balsamic vinegar
3 tbsp chopped coriander (cilantro) leaves
Salt and freshly ground black pepper
White rice, naans or French bread, to serve
Lime wedges, to serve

Heat the oil in large high-sided frying pan or wok over medium heat. When the oil is hot, add the curry leaves and fennel and fenugreek seeds and let the oil take on the flavour of the spices for about 30 seconds while stirring.

Now add the chopped onion and shallots and fry until lightly browned, about 5 minutes. Spoon in the garlic and ginger paste along with the chopped chillies and fry for a further 30 seconds. Add the turmeric and cumin and stir it all up to combine.

Pour in the chopped tomatoes and sauté for about 2 minutes until you have a thick sauce. Add the thick coconut milk, followed by the quartered crabs. Bring to a simmer and then sprinkle in the jaggery or brown sugar. When the crab meat is heated through, add the vinegar and season with salt and pepper to taste.

Stir in the chopped coriander (cilantro) and check the seasoning. Serve with rice, naans or French bread, with lime wedges for squeezing over.

If you can't find the banana leaves, you can cook the salmon in kitchen foil. That said, please try to find the banana leaves as the salmon looks amazing presented at the table all wrapped up in the leaves, and they do give the fish a beautiful flavour.

SALMON FILLET BAKED IN BANANA LEAF

SERVES 4

PREP TIME: 10 MINUTES
COOKING TIME: 15 MINUTES

4 banana leaves, soaked in water
   for about 20 minutes
4 x 250g (9oz) salmon fillets
1 garlic clove, finely chopped
1 tbsp good-quality or
   homemade garam masala
1/2 tsp red chilli powder
1 lemon
Salt and freshly ground black
   pepper
3 tbsp melted butter
3 tbsp finely chopped coriander
   (cilantro) leaves, to serve

Preheat your oven to 200°C/400°F/Gas 6.

Wash the banana leaves well and place them on a work surface with the light side facing upward. Lay a salmon fillet on each leaf and rub the chopped garlic equally into each piece. Mix the garam masala, 1 tsp black pepper and chilli powder, then sprinkle it equally over the salmon fillets. Cut the lemon in half and squeeze the juice from one half of the lemon over the fillets. Cut the other lemon half into thin slices and place the slices on top of the fillets. Add salt and pepper to taste and drizzle with the melted butter.

Wrap the salmon with the banana leaves to form parcels (as pictured). Now place the salmon parcels on a baking tray, with the seams tucked underneath to secure them closed, and bake for about 15 minutes. This should leave the centre of the salmon medium rare, but ovens do vary so you may need to experiment.

When the salmon is cooked, serve each parcel at the table with a bowl of chopped coriander (cilantro) to sprinkle over the top of the fish.

Don't let the fact that there are a lot of ingredients in this one scare you off! This is one of my favourite seafood recipes and it's actually quite easy to make.

SKEWERED HALIBUT CURRY
SERVES 4–6

PREP TIME: 20 MINUTES, PLUS MARINATING
COOKING TIME: 30 MINUTES

1 tbsp rapeseed oil
1kg (2lb 2oz) meaty fish, such as halibut or cod, cut into 5cm (2in) cubes
1 red onion, quartered
1 tsp ground cardamom
1¹⁄₂ tsp ground cinnamon
1 tbsp ground turmeric
1 tbsp chilli powder (or more or less to taste)
1 tbsp dried red chilli (hot pepper) flakes
1 tbsp garam masala
1 tsp salt (more or less to taste)
A handful of green chillies
Rice, to serve

FOR THE SAUCE
1 tbsp rapeseed oil
1 stick of cinnamon
3 cloves
3 green cardamon pods
20 fresh curry leaves (see page 155)
1 red onion, roughly chopped
2 tbsp finely chopped lemongrass
1 thumb-sized piece of ginger, finely sliced
6 garlic cloves, roughly chopped
3 green chillies, roughly chopped (or to taste)
2 tomatoes, roughly chopped
1 tsp finely ground black pepper
1 tsp red chilli powder
1 tsp ground turmeric
400ml (1³⁄₄ cups) coconut milk
Juice of 1 or more limes
Salt

Pre-heat the oven to 180ºC/350ºF/Gas 4.

Start by marinating your fish and onion. Pour the oil over the cubed fish and quartered red onion, then add the ground spices, chilli flakes and salt to taste. Mix it all up and allow to marinate for 10 minutes (and not more than 30 minutes).

Meanwhile, prepare the sauce. Pour the oil into a large pan set over medium–high heat. When it begins to bubble, add the cinnamon stick, cloves and cardamom pods. Fry for about 30 seconds to allow the oil to take on the flavour of the spices, then add the curry leaves, onion, lemongrass and ginger. Cook this until the onion becomes translucent and soft, then add the garlic and green chillies. Let this sizzle for a minute or so, then pour in the chopped tomatoes. Stir this all up nicely to combine and add black pepper, chilli powder and turmeric. Turn up the heat slightly and add the coconut milk. Bring it to a simmer and allow it to thicken slightly.

Skewer the cubed fish, red onion and green chillies and place in a roasting pan. Cover the fish with the sauce and cook for about 15 minutes, or until the fish is cooked through. Season with salt and perhaps a little more black pepper to taste. Squeeze the lime juice over the top. Serve with plain white rice.

< 30 GF

This recipe was sent to me by my friend Milon Miah, Head Chef at Spice Island in Barnard Castle. The recipe was taught to Milon by his mother, but he claims to have modernized it a bit. I've never tried the original but have to say his version, which he makes with chital (a freshwater Bangladeshi fish) is truly delicious. I'm not the only one who thinks so. Milon recently won first place with this dish on the reality TV show 'The Chef'. The ingredients are all very simple but they work so well together. All you need is a little plain white rice and you've got yourself a masterpiece meal in minutes.

SALMON KOFTA BHUNA
SERVES 4

PREP TIME: 15 MINUTES
COOKING TIME: 15 MINUTES

FOR THE KOFTA
500g (1lb 2 oz) salmon fillet or
    chital fish
1 tsp mixed powder (see page 49)
    or curry powder
$\frac{1}{2}$ tsp ground turmeric
1 tsp chilli powder
3 tbsp finely chopped coriander
    (cilantro) leaves
2 spring onions (scallions),
    thinly sliced
$\frac{1}{2}$ tsp salt, or to taste
Oil, for shallow frying

FOR THE SAUCE
2 tbsp rapeseed oil
2 onions, finely chopped
$\frac{1}{2}$ each green and red pepper
    (bell pepper), diced
3 garlic cloves, finely chopped
3 spring onions (scallions),
    roughly chopped
2 green chillies, finely chopped
3 tbsp finely chopped coriander
    (cilantro) leaves
1 tsp ground turmeric
1 tsp chilli powder
1 tbsp mixed powder (see
    page 49) or curry powder
20 cherry tomatoes, cut in half
Salt
Lemon or lime wedges, to serve

In a food processor, blitz the salmon or chital until you have a thick paste. Add the rest of the kofta ingredients, except the oil, and mix well. Set aside.

To make the sauce, heat the rapeseed oil in a large pan over medium–high heat. When visibly hot, stir in the chopped onions and diced peppers and fry until the onions are soft and translucent. Stir in the garlic, spring onions (scallions), chillies, coriander (cilantro) and the ground spices and stir it all up well. Add just enough water to cover and simmer until the water has almost evaporated.

Meanwhile, form the fish paste into about 12 small, flat koftas. In a large frying pan, pour in oil to the depth of about 2.5cm (1in) and heat it over medium–high heat. When hot, add the koftas and fry for about 2 minutes on one side. Flip over and fry for another 2 minutes, or until cooked through.

Place the tomatoes and koftas on top of the simmering sauce for a couple of minutes until the tomatoes are warmed through. Season with salt to taste.

To serve, divide the sauce mixture equally between four warmed plates. Place three koftas on each and serve with wedges of lemon or lime.

This is a light and delicious fish dish that is often seen on starter menus but works really well as a main dish too. It's really easy to make, but you'd never know it from all the fantastic flavours. This recipe was sent to me by Zulfi Karim, owner of Curryosity near Bradford. Zulfi uses haddock but lately I've been making this dish with my favourite fish, halibut. It might be a little more expensive than haddock but I love the meaty texture. You could also use cod for this recipe.

You can use whole fillets of fish or cut them into bite-sized pieces. I like to serve this dish with my spicy coriander, coconut and chilli chutney with about five tablespoons of plain yoghurt whisked into it (see page 141).

MASALA MACHLI
SERVES 4 OR MORE AS PART OF A MULTI-COURSE MEAL

PREP TIME: 10 MINUTES, PLUS MARINATING
COOKING TIME: 6 MINUTES

700g (1lb 9oz) halibut, cod or haddock
3 tbsp lemon juice
2 tbsp plain (all-purpose) flour
4 tbsp cornflour (cornstarch)
1 tbsp ground tumeric
3 tbsp garam masala
2 tbsp ajwain seeds
2 tbsp tandoori masala
2 tsp chilli powder
1 tsp crushed chilli (hot pepper) flakes
$\frac{1}{2}$ tsp salt
Rapeseed oil, for frying
Coriander chutney or tomato salsa, to serve

Marinate the fish in the lemon juice in a non-metallic bowl for no more than 10 minutes.

While the fish is marinating, mix the flours, dried spices and salt together in a large bowl. Turn the marinated fish pieces in the flour mixture to coat then shake off any excess. There only needs to be a thin dusting of the flour mixture on the fish.

Heat about 2.5cm (1in) depth of rapeseed oil in a large frying pan. Place the fish in the oil and cook for about 2 minutes. Then, flip the fish over and cook for another 1 minute on the other side, or until just cooked through.

Serve the fish with the above mentioned coriander chutney or tomato salsa (see page 142), which also goes really well.

QUICK VEGETARIAN CURRIES AND SIDE DISHES

Really, with a bit of creativity, any of the meat curries in this book could be adapted to be served vegetarian. Use the freshest produce you can get your hands on and go for it. I like to experiment with vegetable koftas, like those in my Malai kofta curry on page 84. Different vegetables could be stirred into the koftas to vary them in appearance and flavour. These can be stirred into and served with your sauces of choice.

Try the tasty selection of vegetarian dishes I have for you here and let your imagination run wild. You might be surprised at all the delicious combos you can come up with.

I promise, you won't miss the meat when you make these koftas. Served in the mildly spice, creamy sauce, they are real crowd pleasers! The koftas could also be made smaller and flattened into patties so you don't need to cook with as much oil.

MALAI KOFTA CURRY
SERVES 4 OR MORE AS PART OF A MULTI-COURSE MEAL

PREP TIME: 20 MINUTES
COOKING TIME: 40 MINUTES

250g (9oz) peeled potatoes
1 tbsp rice flour (see page 155)
1 tbsp plain (all-purpose) flour
   (or an additional 1 tbsp rice
   flour, if going gluten free)
200g (7oz) paneer (see
   page 155), grated
1 tsp ground turmeric
2 tsp chilli powder
1 large handful baby spinach
   leaves, washed and chopped
4 tbsp chopped coriander
   (cilantro) leaves
$\frac{1}{2}$ tsp salt
Rapeseed or vegetable oil,
   for deep frying
Garam masala, to serve

FOR THE SAUCE

4 tbsp rapeseed or vegetable oil
1 tbsp ground cumin
1 tbsp ground coriander
10 almonds
10 cashews
2 onions, finely chopped
2 green chillies, finely chopped
2 tbsp mixed garlic and ginger
   paste (see page 7)
400g (14oz) can chopped
   tomatoes
200ml ($\frac{3}{4}$ cup) single (light)
   cream
Salt

Start by making your koftas. Par-cook the potatoes for 5 minutes until almost cooked through – it should be easy to stick a fork in but there should still be some resistance. Remove the potatoes from the water and allow to cool, and then grate them. Squeeze as much moisture as possible from the grated potatoes and mix with the rice and plain (all-purpose) flours. Let stand for about 5 minutes.

Mix the grated paneer, $\frac{1}{2}$ teaspoon of the turmeric, 1 teaspoon of the chilli powder, the chopped spinach and coriander (cilantro) into the grated potato. To this add the salt. Form into koftas slightly larger than golf balls and set aside while you make your sauce.

Heat the oil in a large saucepan over medium–high heat. When visibly hot, stir in the remaining turmeric and chilli powder and the cumin, ground coriander, almonds and cashews. Temper this all in the oil for about 30 seconds, then add the chopped onions. Fry for about 5 minutes until soft and translucent.

Add the green chillies and the garlic and ginger paste and fry for a further 1 minute, then add the tomatoes. Simmer for about 5 minutes and then blend to a smooth sauce using a hand-held or countertop blender. Return this to the pan and add about 400ml ($1\frac{3}{4}$ cups) water and simmer down for about 15 minutes. Stir in the cream and continue to simmer until you are happy with the consistency. Season with salt to taste and keep warm.

You can fry your koftas while the sauce is simmering if time is an issue. To cook the koftas, heat about 10cm (4in) depth of rapeseed or vegetable oil in a saucepan – you need enough oil in your pan to just cover the koftas so add more if required. The oil is hot enough for frying when a small piece broken off one of the koftas sizzles and rises to the top immediately when thrown into the oil. Carefully place your koftas in the oil and fry until crispy brown on the exterior. About 5 minutes should do the trick. Don't overcrowd your pan. Do this in batches if necessary.

Place the fried koftas on paper towels to soak up excess oil and then place in a large or individual serving bowls and cover with the sauce. Sprinkle with garam masala and a drizzle of cream to serve.

Put simply, cauliflower never tasted so good. The double frying technique makes it easier to prepare ahead and gets those cauliflower nuggets extra crispy.

MANCHURIAN GOBI

SERVES 4 OR MORE AS PART OF A MULTI-COURSE MEAL

PREP TIME: 15 MINUTES, PLUS MARINATING
COOKING TIME: 20 MINUTES

About 750g (1lb 10oz) cauliflower, broken into florets
1 tsp ground turmeric
Rapeseed oil, for frying

FOR THE MARINADE
2 tbsp mixed garlic and ginger paste (see page 7)
1 tsp red chilli powder
2 tsp ground black pepper
Salt

FOR THE BATTER
125g (1 cup) plain (all-purpose) flour
30g (¼ cup) cornflour (cornstarch)
40g (¼ cup) rice flour (see page 155) (or more cornflour)

FOR THE SAUCE
2 tbsp rapeseed oil or sesame oil
2 red onions, finely chopped
5 garlic cloves, thinly sliced
2.5cm (1in) piece of ginger, finely chopped
3 green chillies, finely chopped
125ml (½ cup) plain passata (sieved tomatoes), or blended chopped tomatoes
2–3 tbsp hot sauce (for homemade see page 143)
1 tbsp light soy sauce
1 tbsp white wine vinegar or coconut vinegar
1 heaped tbsp sugar (optional)
4 spring onions (scallions), sliced, plus extra to serve
2 tbsp chopped coriander (cilantro) leaves

Bring 1 litre (4 cups) of lightly salted water to a rapid boil, then turn off the heat. Add the cauliflower and turmeric and let the cauliflower cook in the hot water for about 3 minutes. Drain and transfer the par-cooked cauliflower to a clean kitchen towel and dry. The turmeric can stain so don't use one of your best towels.

Once dry, mix together the marinade ingredients and rub the marinade all over the cauliflower. Let rest for about 20 minutes, or longer. This can all be done ahead of time.

When ready to cook, make the batter. Mix the batter ingredients well in a mixing bowl and add just enough water to make a thick batter. It should be pourable but it needs to be thick enough to coat the cauliflower. Add the cauliflower florets to the batter so that they are all nicely coated.

Now heat about 10cm (4in) depth of rapeseed oil in a large pan over medium–high heat. The oil is hot enough when a small piece of battered cauliflower sizzles immediately when dropped in the oil. Fry the battered cauliflower for about 3 minutes until lightly browned. I usually do this in batches so that I don't overcrowd the pan. Transfer the cooked cauliflower to paper towels to cool while you cook the rest of the cauliflower. Now turn up the heat to high and fry the cauliflower again for another 2–3 minutes until crispy and golden brown. This double frying makes the cauliflower nice and crispy.

To make the sauce, heat the 2 tablespoons rapeseed oil in a large frying pan over medium–high heat and sauté the chopped onion for about 5 minutes until soft and translucent. Add the chopped garlic, ginger and chillies and fry for a further 30 seconds. Now pour in the passata (sieved tomatoes) and hot sauce, soy sauce, vinegar and sugar, if using. Allow to simmer for a couple of minutes, then stir in the chopped spring onions (scallions) and cauliflower. Mix well so that the cauliflower is evenly coated with the sauce.

To serve, check for seasoning and sprinkle with a little more chopped spring onions and the coriander (cilantro) to serve.

I whip this one up for lunch all the time because it's so quick and easy to prepare. It's also good for you and tastes delicious, so that's a bonus. For ease and convenience, I have used canned kidney beans in this recipe. If you have the time and the will, you will get better results using an equal amount of dried, soaked and cooked kidney beans. Just follow the instructions on the bag.

KIDNEY BEAN CURRY
SERVES 4 OR MORE AS PART OF A MULTI-COURSE MEAL

PREP TIME: 5 MINUTES
COOKING TIME: 25 MINUTES

1 large onion, chopped
3 tbsp ghee or rapeseed oil
2 tbsp mixed garlic and ginger
    paste (see page 7)
1–3 green chillies, finely
    chopped (to taste)
1 tsp ground cumin
250ml (1 cup) tomato plain
    passata (sieved tomatoes)
    or blended canned tomatoes
2 x 400g (14oz) cans of kidney
    beans, drained
Salt
1 tsp garam masala, to serve
Freshly chopped coriander
    (cilantro) leaves, to serve

Place your chopped onion in a blender with just enough water to blend to a thick paste.

Heat the ghee or rapeseed oil in a large saucepan over medium–high heat. Pour in the onion paste and fry for about 15 minutes until it is quite dark brown in colour. Add the garlic and ginger paste along with the chopped chillies and cumin and stir to combine.

Pour in the passata (sieved tomatoes) and bring to a bubble. Simmer for about 5–10 minutes until the sauce is quite thick. Pour in the kidney beans and continue cooking until heated through. Season with salt to taste and sprinkle with the garam masala and chopped coriander (cilantro) to serve.

I love cauliflower. I remember when I was a kid and the stuff used to send me running. I brought my kids up on it so they have always liked what could be referred to as a rather boring vegetable. This recipe is anything but boring. There is so much going on. From the tempered spices to the crunchy coconut flakes and almonds, this dish simply gets it. It is important to cut the florets quite small so that they cook quickly when stir fried. If you're looking for a nice side dish to enjoy with your next curry, or you want a main course vegetarian dish, this one ticks all the boxes.

STIR-FRIED CAULIFLOWER
WITH ALMONDS AND COCONUT

SERVES 4 OR MORE AS PART OF A MULTI-COURSE MEAL

PREP TIME: 10 MINUTES
COOKING TIME: 20 MINUTES

3 tbsp rapeseed oil
1 tsp black mustard seeds
1 tsp cumin seeds
10 fresh or frozen curry leaves (see page 155)
2 onions, finely chopped
2 green chillies, finely chopped
5 garlic cloves, cut into thin slivers
1 large handful flaked (slivered) almonds
1 large handful coconut flakes
1/2 tsp ground turmeric
1 head of cauliflower, cut into small florets
Salt
1/2 tsp garam masala, to serve
Chopped coriander (cilantro) leaves, to serve

Heat the oil in a large frying pan over high heat. When visibly hot, add the mustard seeds and fry until they begin to pop. Lower the heat to medium and stir in the cumin seeds and curry leaves. Temper all these spices and herbs in the hot oil for about 30 seconds, then toss in the chopped onions. Fry for about 5 minutes until soft and translucent, then stir in the green chillies and garlic. Continue cooking for another minute or so, then add the flaked (slivered) almonds. Toast them in the hot oil for a couple of minutes and then add the coconut flakes. Toast these with the almonds for another couple of minutes until toasty brown.

Stir in the turmeric, add the cauliflower and fry for about 3 minutes. Add about 100ml (scant 1/2 cup) of water and cook, covered, for about 3 minutes more. Remove the lid and continue moving the cauliflower around in the pan until it is cooked through but still has a bit of bite to it. Season with salt to taste and sprinkle with the garam masala and fresh coriander (cilantro) to serve.

Cauliflower rice is a delicious alternative to rice. Just think... no soaking or steaming. This is a straight forward stir-fry dish that can be served on its own as a main or as a side dish with a good curry. The soy sauce is a nice touch. If you are on a gluten-free diet, use coconut amino as most soy sauces contain gluten.

CAULIFLOWER EGG FRIED 'RICE'
SERVES 4 OR MORE AS PART OF A MULTI-COURSE MEAL

PREP TIME: 15 MINUTES
COOKING TIME: 15 MINUTES

1 head cauliflower, cut into florets
3 tbsp rapeseed oil
2 large eggs
4 spring onions (scallions), thinly sliced
2 tbsp mixed garlic and ginger paste (see page 7)
1 carrot, finely diced
70g (½ cup) peas, fresh or frozen
1 red pepper (bell pepper), finely chopped
2 green chillies, finely chopped (optional)
3 tbsp flaked (slivered) almonds
2–3 tbsp coconut amino (see page 155) or soy sauce
Salt and freshly ground black pepper

Using a food processor, pulse the cauliflower until it resembles rice.

Heat 1 tablespoon of the oil in a large pan over medium–high heat. Now, whisk the eggs and pour them into the pan. Scramble the eggs, then remove them to a chopping board and cut into small pieces.

Wipe the pan clean and add the remaining oil. Add the chopped spring onions (scallions), garlic and ginger and sauté until fragrant, about 30 seconds. Stir in the carrot and sauté until tender but still quite crisp, about 2 minutes. Add the peas, red pepper (bell pepper), green chillies (if using) and the cauliflower 'rice' to the pan, stirring to combine all the ingredients.

Lower the heat to medium, cover the pan and cook until the cauliflower rice is tender, about 5 minutes. Uncover and stir in the eggs, flaked (slivered) almonds and coconut amino or soy sauce. Check for seasoning and serve immediately.

TIP: Prepared cauliflower rice is now available at most supermarkets for convenience.

This is really just a quick stir fry with rice. It's a biryani like you find at most curry houses, as it is so easy and fast to prepare. You could also add cooked meat, like chicken or lamb, to the mushrooms or substitute the meat for the mushrooms. If you happen to have some base curry sauce made (see pages 50 and 51) you could stir in a ladle or so to give it more sauce, but this is usually served quite dry. If you do add sauce, be sure to adjust the seasoning to taste. Serve with a raita and/or hot sauce spooned over the top.

QUICK MUSHROOM BIRYANI
SERVES 4 OR MORE AS PART OF A MULTI-COURSE MEAL

PREP TIME: 15 MINUTES, PLUS COOKING AND CHILLING THE RICE
COOKING TIME: 15 MINUTES

3 tbsp milk
A pinch of saffron
2 tbsp rapeseed oil
5cm (2in) cinnamon stick
5 cloves
6 black peppercorns
4 green cardamom pods, bruised
2 bay leaves
1 large onion, finely chopped
2 tomatoes, finely chopped
1 tbsp mixed garlic and ginger
    paste (see page 7)
2 green chillies, finely chopped
1 tbsp ground cumin
200g (7oz) button mushrooms,
    thinly sliced
1 x recipe quantity steamed white
    rice (see page 149), chilled
1 tsp garam masala (optional)
1 small bunch of coriander
    (cilantro), finely chopped
Salt and freshly ground black
    pepper
Raita and hot sauce, to serve

First, heat your milk to hand hot, but not boiling, and then sprinkle the saffron in it to infuse while you make the rest of the dish.

Heat the oil in a large high-sided frying pan until visibly hot. Throw in the cinnamon, cloves, black peppercorns, cardamom pods and bay leaves and let the oil soak up their awesome flavour for about 30 seconds.

Now toss in the chopped onion and fry for about 5 minutes until the onion is soft and translucent. Add the chopped tomatoes and cook for a further 1 minute or so before adding the garlic and ginger paste and the chopped chillies. Stir well to combine, then add the cumin and mushrooms and cook them through until hot and soft. Stir in the cold rice and coat with the oil and other ingredients. Stir regularly to ensure the rice is good and hot but be careful not to stir too vigorously or the rice will split.

To finish, pour the saffron infused milk over the top and sprinkle with garam masala and chopped coriander (cilantro). Season with salt to taste. I like to serve this biryani topped with coriander raita (see page 139) and homemade hot sauce (see page 143).

This is a recipe I developed last minute for a Sunday morning food demo. It was right after my first book was published and I was cooking at quite a few food festivals at the time. I returned home late one Saturday evening to find my 18-year-old son drinking beer and serving up a feast to friends with all the prepared ingredients I needed for the following morning. I could have killed him but that would have been illegal! Fortunately, I still had enough chicken and base sauce for the chicken tikka masala I had planned but the chicken jalfrezi wasn't going to happen. I had the following ingredients on hand and decided to make this restaurant-style chilli paneer.

CHILLI PANEER STIR FRY
SERVES 4 OR MORE AS PART OF A MULTI-COURSE MEAL

PREP TIME: 10 MINUTES,
PLUS MARINATING
COOKING TIME: 15 MINUTES

250g (9oz) paneer (see
    page 155), cubed
2 tbsp rapeseed oil, plus extra
1 tbsp unsalted butter
10 fresh or frozen curry leaves
    (see page 155)
1 heaped tbsp mixed garlic and
    ginger paste (see page 7)
$^1/_2$ red pepper (bell pepper),
    diced
$^1/_2$ green pepper (bell pepper),
    diced
2 green chillies, finely chopped
1 tbsp mixed powder (see
    page 49) or curry powder
1 tsp chilli powder
1 tbsp ground black pepper
Juice of 1 lime
Salt

FOR THE MARINADE
1 tbsp rice flour (see page 155)
    or cornflour (cornstarch)
2 tbsp plain (all-purpose) flour
$^1/_2$ tsp chilli powder
$^1/_2$ tsp ground turmeric
1 tsp mixed powder (see
    page 49) or garam masala
1 heaped tbsp mixed garlic and
    ginger paste (see page 7)

Mix the marinade ingredients into a paste with $^1/_2$ teaspoon salt. Make a few small holes in each piece of paneer with a fork and then cover the paneer pieces with the marinade. Let them marinate for at least 20 minutes, or overnight.

When ready to cook, heat the oil in a large pan. When visibly hot, add the marinated paneer and brown on each side until you have a batch of beautifully browned paneer cubes. Transfer to a plate while you make the sauce.

Add a little more oil to the pan, if needed, and the butter. Heat it up over medium–high heat and then stir in the curry leaves. Let them sizzle for about 30 seconds until fragrant, then stir in the garlic and ginger paste, (bell) peppers and chillies. Stir to coat in the oil, then add the ground spices. Pour in about 100ml (scant $^1/_2$ cup) water and bring to a simmer. Add the fried paneer and stir it into the sauce. Simmer until most of the water has evaporated and the cheese is heated through. Squeeze the lime juice over the top, season with salt to taste and serve.

It's so often the case that the best recipes are the simplest. You don't need to slave over the hob all day to make a delicious meal. Back in 2015, I visited Thali on Old Brompton Road in London. I was there to review the restaurant and they brought out a meal that was beyond amazing.

One of the side dishes they served that evening was this saag paneer. This wasn't a dish I would normally order, but I loved it! So much so, I asked them for the recipe. This is my play on their amazing recipe. You will need a big pan for this one as there is so much spinach, but it does reduce down a lot during cooking. You could also use frozen spinach for this recipe, which is a lot easier.

SAAG PANEER

SERVES 4 OR MORE AS PART OF A MULTI-COURSE MEAL

PREP TIME: 10 MINUTES
COOKING TIME: 20 MINUTES

250g (9oz) paneer (see page 155), cubed
5 tbsp rapeseed oil
800g (1³/₄lb) fresh baby spinach leaves, or 450g (1lb) frozen spinach
1 tsp cumin seeds
1 tsp red chilli powder (or more or less to taste – optional)
1 tsp ground turmeric
4 fat garlic cloves, finely chopped
2 tbsp plain yoghurt
Salt
3 tbsp single (light) cream (optional)

FOR THE PANEER MARINADE
¹/₂ tsp ground turmeric
¹/₂ tsp chilli powder
¹/₂ tsp salt
1 tsp rapeseed oil

With a fork, make a few holes in each paneer cube and then mix well with the marinade ingredients. You can fry these immediately but the paneer does benefit from a longer marinating time.

Fry the paneer in about 3 tablespoons of the oil in a frying pan set over medium–high heat until nicely browned. Set aside while you cook the spinach.

Pour in 285ml water (10fl oz) into a large saucepan and bring to the boil. Add the spinach and simmer until the water has evaporated. Allow the spinach to cool, then blitz to a thick paste in a food processor. Set aside.

Now heat the remaining oil in a large frying pan over medium–high heat. When visibly hot, add the cumin seeds and stir them around in the oil for about 30 seconds, then add the chilli powder and turmeric. Stir in the chopped garlic and fry until it is light golden brown in colour. Be careful not to burn the garlic or it will turn bitter.

Add the blended spinach to the pan and stir in the yoghurt, 1 tablespoon at a time. Stir in the fried paneer and heat through. Season with salt to taste and serve immediately. I like to stir in about 3 tablespoons of single cream to finish the dish off. This is optional but very nice.

I was introduced to pav bhaji by my friend and award-winning chef, Syed Ahmed, of Duke Bombay Café in Darlington. I love the food that comes out of his kitchen and this buttery pav bhaji is one of my all-time favourites. Authentic pav bhaji is cooked with a lot of butter. If you aren't keen on using the amount of butter I suggest here, you can of course reduce the amount.

PAV BHAJI
SERVES 4

PREP TIME: 15 MINUTES
COOKING TIME: 25 MINUTES

FOR THE VEGETABLES
2 large potatoes, peeled and
    finely sliced
250g (9oz) cauliflower florets
1 small carrot, peeled and diced
100g (³/₄ cup) fresh or frozen
    peas
400g (14oz) canned chopped
    tomatoes
Salt

**FOR THE MASALA (SPICY
SAUCE MIXTURE)**
200g (³/₄ cup) unsalted butter
1 large red onion (about
    250g/9oz), finely chopped
1 tsp cumin seeds
1 tbsp red chilli powder
    (more or less to taste)
¹/₂ tsp ground turmeric
4 fat garlic cloves, grated
2.5cm (1in) piece of ginger,
    peeled and grated
1 red pepper (bell pepper),
    finely chopped
1 tbsp garam masala
Salt

TO SERVE
Ladi pav (see page 152) or
    shop-bought soft buns
Butter, for spreading
Coriander (cilantro) leaves
4 lemon wedges
1 red onion, finely chopped

Put the sliced potatoes, cauliflower, carrot, peas and chopped tomatoes in a large pot and add just enough water to cover. Bring to the boil and cover with a lid. Cook for about 20 minutes, stirring occasionally until the potato and vegetables are soft. Using a potato masher, mash it all up. It should be a bit wetter than mashed potato consistency – like creamy and slightly chunky potato soup – so add a drop of water if needed. Season with salt to taste and keep warm.

Melt about 100g (7 tbsp) of the butter in a large frying pan over medium–high heat. Toss in the chopped onion and cumin seeds and fry until the onion is soft. Now add the chilli powder, turmeric, garlic, ginger and red pepper (bell pepper) and fry for a further 1 minute or so. Stir in the garam masala, season with salt to taste. Whisk this mixture into your mashed vegetables. Top with the remaining butter and allow to melt.

To serve, cut the rolls in half and butter them generously on both sides. Place them, butter-side down, in a hot frying pan to brown them. Place the toasted buns on warmed plates with a good helping of the bhaji. Sprinkle with chopped coriander (cilantro) and serve with lemon wedges and finely chopped red onion on the side.

Dhal makhani, when cooked correctly, is delicious. I've tried some amazing versions and also a few that just weren't quite there yet. If you like a good dhal makhani, I think this recipe will get you the flavour and texture you're looking for. Be warned, however, this isn't one you can just whip up on a whim. The lentils need to soak in water for at least 12 hours, then be slowly cooked until fall-apart tender. This is where many chefs go wrong. They rush the cooking process and the dhal has just a bit too much bite to it. If time permits, I recommend cooking this for four hours adding water when required.

DHAL MAKHANI

SERVES 4 OR MORE AS PART OF A MULTI-COURSE MEAL

PREP TIME: 10 MINUTES, PLUS SOAKING
COOKING TIME: 2–4 HOURS

200g (1 cup) black urad dhal lentils (see page 155), soaked overnight in cold water
5 tbsp rapeseed oil
2 onions, finely chopped
2 tbsp mixed garlic and ginger paste (see page 7)
2 tomatoes, chopped
2 tsp chilli powder
1 tsp ground turmeric
1 tbsp garam masala
1 tsp paprika
2 tsp salt, or to taste
3 tbsp butter, or to taste
250ml (1 cup) single (light) cream
Chopped coriander (cilantro) leaves, to serve

In a large saucepan over low–medium heat, simmer the urad dhal lentils in water until fall-apart soft. You might need to top up the water from time to time while the lentils cook. After about 3–4 hours of simmering, the lentils will be perfectly soft. Strain the lentils, reserving the cooking water, and set it all aside.

To save time, the following steps can be done while your lentils are simmering. Heat the oil in a large frying pan over medium–high heat. When visibly hot, stir in the chopped onions and fry for about 10 minutes until soft and lightly browned. Stir in the garlic and ginger paste and fry for about 30 seconds before adding the chopped tomatoes and the spices. Cook for another minute, then add about 125ml (½ cup) of the strained lentil water. Bring this to a simmer and add the cooked lentils. Cook over high heat for 5 minutes, adding more strained water if needed. The dhal should be thick and soupy.

To finish, season with salt to taste. I recommend about 2 teaspoons, which I think works really well, but as with all the recipes in this book, I feel how much salt you add is a personal thing. Add it to taste. Makhani means butter so you can't leave that out. I recommend using about 3 tablespoons but if you don't want to use that much, the dhal will still be delicious. Stir most of it into the dhal and then top with whatever is leftover to melt on top. Drizzle the cream over the top and sprinkle with the chopped coriander (cilantro) and you are ready to serve your masterpiece.

I love masala chips. Whether I'm serving them as a main dish or doing what I normally do, serving them as a side, they are always a big hit. This is especially so since I started using this recipe that was shown to me by my friend Alfarid 'Billy' Juma, owner of the Choma Grill House in Preston. The recipe couldn't be easier, but you've got to follow the instructions carefully – there is a reason Billy's masala chips are the talk of the town. This is true comfort food and I promise you that if you have one chip in his special masala sauce, you'll find it difficult to stop. For ease and economy, most chip shops use frozen chips. I prefer this recipe with deep-fried chips but you could also use oven-baked chips.

MASALA CHIPS
SERVES 4 OR MORE AS PART OF A MULTI-COURSE MEAL

PREP TIME: 10 MINUTES
COOKING TIME: 20 MINUTES

900g (2lb) frozen chips (preferably the kind you deep fry, but oven bake will do)
Rapeseed or vegetable oil, for deep frying
1 tsp red chilli powder
½ tsp ground cumin
1 tsp ground coriander
Salt

FOR THE MASALA SAUCE
2 tbsp rapeseed oil
1 tbsp cumin seeds
5 tbsp tomato hamburger relish
5 tbsp ketchup
1 tbsp sugar
½ onion, finely chopped
1 tbsp mixed garlic and ginger paste (see page 7)

First make the sauce. Heat the oil in a saucepan over medium–high heat. When visibly hot, stir in the cumin seeds and sauté in the oil for about 30 seconds until fragrant. Add the hamburger relish followed by the ketchup and bring to simmer. Stir in the sugar and continue to cook for about 1 minute, then add the chopped onion and garlic and ginger paste and stir it all up to combine. Season with a little salt and take off the heat while your prepare your chips.

Cook your chips as per the instructions on the packet. Most takeaways use frozen chips that they deep fry. I highly recommend doing the same, but if you're looking for a lighter or less messy option, oven chips will do. When your chips are ready, season them directly with the chilli powder, cumin, coriander and a little bit of salt to taste. Remember there is already some salt in the masala sauce, so go easy.

While the chips are still hot, begin adding them to the pan with the sauce, stirring so that every chip is evenly covered in the sauce. Ideally, the process of coating the chips in the sauce and serving should be done in a couple of minutes. If you let them sit too long, the chips will get soggy rather than the crispy sauce-coated chips they are.

UTTAPAMS, IDLIS AND DOSAS

Uttapams, idlis and dosas are finding their way onto many new curry house menus. These are specialties of southern India and with more Indian-run curry restaurants becoming increasingly popular, people are discovering and falling in love with them. So many people have said to me that they wish they could make dosas at home. Well now you can.

Dosas might be a bit difficult to make at first but they get easier with practice. Think about Pancake Day... The first few pancakes almost always look a bit of a mess. Just as everyone has had their fill, you're turning them out like a professional! So, I didn't want to leave them out just because this is a cookbook of 'easy' recipes! Make yourself some batter (see pages 104 or 105) and try uttapams and idlis first (see my notes below). I've included a few popular ways of serving them that I hope will inspire you to search for or even invent a few of your own recipes. Then, move on to crispy dosas.

ADVICE FOR DOSA NOVICES

I have watched dosas being made at many restaurants. There is the traditional way of spreading a little oil over a large crêpe maker with half an onion. Crêpe makers are rarely non-stick and the oil and onion juice helps ensure the dosa doesn't stick to the surface. The best advice I received for beginners was from my friend and head chef of The Curry Café in Brighton, Sabu Joseph. He suggests using a non-stick pan and getting it really hot. Then he cools the surface down with a cold, wet towel and quickly spreads his batter. Although I love the large dosas I can make using my crêpe maker, go for the non-stick option if you are new to this. As the pan is non-stick, you don't even need any oil.

NOTES FROM MY KITCHEN TESTS:

★ Both batters on the following pages will work well for dosas, idlis and uttapams but for best results, you need to whisk in $1/2$ teaspoon baking powder if making idlis or uttapams using the cheat's method. Don't use baking powder for dosas.

★ Making my cheat's batter will save you money but there are really good commercial dosa, idli and uttapam instant batters available at Asian shops and some supermarkets. It may be worth noting that some of the packaged batters are not gluten free. If using a packet batter, follow the instructions on the packet.

★ The cheat's batter is ready to use when mixed. However, just like making sour dough, the batter will benefit in flavour from fermenting overnight. Another option is to add a squeeze of lemon to the batter, which will work as a delicious souring agent.

★ When fermenting the authentic batter, I find that placing it in my oven with just the light switched on works really well. You want the inside of your oven to be warm but not at all hot, like a warm spring day. Of course in the warmer months, you could also just place the batter in a warm location.

★ Non-stick pans are best for beginners to make dosas. If using an electric crêpe maker that isn't non-stick, set it to 180°C/350°F. Before spreading the batter, rub about 1 teaspoon rapeseed oil over the surface using half an onion so that your dosa doesn't stick. You can cook on a hotter surface once you get used to making dosas.

★ If when you make your dosas the batter clumps, the heat is too high. Go ahead and cook the dosa. It won't look like much but it will still taste good. Perfect dosas come with practice.

(< 30) (GF) (V)

Believe it or not, most dosas, idlis and uttapams served at busy restaurants are made with a flour batter similar to this one. It is a lot less work, cheaper and much faster too. There's no need to ferment the batter, but if you've ever tried dosas, idlis and uttapams using a fermented batter like my recipe on page 105, you will notice the difference. See my test kitchen notes on page 103 before starting this recipe.

You can purchase dosa, uttapam and idli mixes at most Asian grocers and online. This recipe can be used for dosas but you need to include the ¹/₂ teaspoon baking powder if making idlis or uttapams.

DOSA, IDLI AND UTTAPAM BATTER CHEAT'S METHOD

SERVES 4

PREP TIME: 5 MINUTES

200g (1¹/₄ cup) rice flour (see
    page 155)
70g (¹/₂ cup) urad dhal flour
¹/₈ tsp ground fenugreek
1 tsp salt
¹/₂ tsp baking powder (for idlis
    and uttapams only)
410ml (1³/₄ cups) water
Juice of 1 lemon

Pour the flours, ground fenugreek, salt and baking powder, if using, into a bowl. Slowly pour in the water, mixing until you have a thick and smooth batter. The batter should be thick enough to coat the back of a spoon. Use the batter as required in the following recipes.

At first, you might find that making dosas is a bit difficult, but with a little practice you will get them right every time. I recommend starting with idlis and uttapams and working your way up to dosas. That way you can still get the delicious flavour of the fermented batter but not feel under pressure to rise to the challenge of crispy dosas until you're good and ready. If you like dosas as much as I do, you might want to invest in a crêpe maker as you can set the heat to 180°C/350°F, which I have found to be the perfect heat for making dosas. A good non-stick crêpe pan or frying pan is the best choice for beginners. You need to start this recipe 32 hours before you cook, as the batter needs time to ferment.

AUTHENTIC BATTER FOR DOSAS, UTTAPAMS AND IDLIS

MAKES ENOUGH TO SERVE 10–12 PEOPLE

PREP TIME: 25 MINUTES, PLUS SOAKING AND FERMENTING TIME

600g (3¹/₃ cups) broken basmati rice (see page 155) or normal basmati rice
150g (³/₄ cup) white split urad dhal lentils (see page 155)
1 heaped tsp fenugreek seeds
2 tsp sugar
2 tsp sea salt
3 tbsp rapeseed oil

Combine the broken rice, lentils and fenugreek seeds in a large bowl and rinse and drain three times with water. Pour enough warm water into the bowl to cover and soak for 12 hours or overnight.

When ready to make your batter, drain the water completely. Fill a jug with 600ml (2¹/₂ cups) water. Put about a quarter of the soaked rice and lentil mix into a food processor with about 150ml (²/₃ cup) of the water and blend for at least 2 minutes until very smooth. If you rub the batter between your fingers, it should feel smooth and just slightly sandy. Blend longer if needed as blenders do vary. You do not want to rush this. It is an essential part of making the batter.

Transfer the prepared batter to a large bowl and repeat with the rest of the rice and lentil mixture until it is all blended into a batter. Try not to use more than the 600ml (2¹/₂ cups) of water. If you are running low on water at the end and need more liquid to blend, add some of the prepared batter.

Whisk the sugar into your batter and cover with cling film (plastic wrap). The sugar will help the batter ferment and become very tasty. Now place the batter in a warm place to ferment for 24 hours. Please see my notes on page 103.

After 24 hours, the batter should be foamy on the top. Whisk in the salt. Your batter can be kept in an airtight container in the fridge for up to 3 days and it also freezes well. If not using immediately, you will need to whisk it into a smooth batter again before using.

Uttapams are essentially fat dosas. They're thick like American pancakes and often have onions, peppers (bell peppers) and other fresh vegetables cooked into the batter so that they resemble a pizza without all the cheese. You really can't go wrong with them. We're talking south Indian cooking at its easiest! If all you ever make with the batter on page 104 or 105 is uttapams, I think you'll never tire of them. These are delicious served with a selection of tasty dips.

If you're feeling adventurous and you're using the fermented batter (see page 105), try spreading the batter out until it is really thin and you've got yourself a dosa. I give instructions on how to do this in my masala dosa recipe (see page 115) but there's no reason you can't have a play with it before progressing to that recipe. Even if you don't get the batter spread out thinly enough to be considered a dosa, you'll still end up with something in between an uttapam and a dosa and it will taste great.

UTTAPAMS

SERVES 4–5

PREP TIME: 10 MINUTES, PLUS MAKING THE BATTER
COOKING TIME: 6 MINUTES

2 tbsp coconut or rapeseed oil
1/2 red onion, finely sliced
2 green chillies, finely sliced
1/2 red pepper (bell pepper), thinly sliced
2 tomatoes, finely sliced
1/2 recipe quantity authentic batter (see page 105), or a whole batch of cheat's batter (see page 104)
Coconut butter or butter, to serve
Salt and freshly ground black pepper

In a frying pan or crêpe pan, heat the oil over medium–high heat. When visibly hot, add the sliced vegetables. Allow to fry for about 1 minute to soften, then pour a ladle of batter over them. The uttapam should be quite thick, like an American pancake.

Fry until browned on the under-side and sprinkle with black pepper, if you like. Flip over to brown the other side. Keep warm while you make the remaining uttapams.

Serve the uttapams with coconut butter or butter and a little salt to taste. You may not need any additional salt as there is already salt in the dosa batter. I like to serve these with sambar (see page 111), coriander, coconut and chilli chutney (see page 141) and 40-garlic-clove chutney (see page 139) or ginger chutney (see page 140).

To make idlis you will need idli moulds for the best results. These are available online and also at many Asian markets. They aren't expensive and if you enjoy cooking, you will love having them on hand so that you can eat idlis whenever you want! Before I broke down and invested in an idli mould set, I greased and then filled a Yorkshire pudding tray with batter and placed it on a brick in a large lidded pot of boiling water to steam. It worked well so do what you have to to try this recipe. You'll be glad you did.

Fluffy steamed idlis taste great. They are delicious dipped into your favourite chutneys and sambar. I find them exceptionally good shallow fried in a little rapeseed oil or coconut oil and then seasoned to taste with salt.

IDLIS

SERVES 6 OR MORE AS PART OF A MULTI-COURSE MEAL

**PREP TIME: 5 MINUTES,
PLUS MAKING THE BATTER
COOKING TIME: 20 MINUTES**

$^1/_2$ recipe quantity authentic batter (see page 105), or a whole batch of cheat's batter (see page 104)
Vegetable or rapeseed oil, for greasing
Chutneys or sambar, to serve (optional)

When ready to cook, pour about 7.5cm (3in) depth of water into the bottom of your idli pan and bring to the boil. You want the water level to be just below the idli trays so you might need to adjust the amount of water you use depending on your pan. Oil your idli trays lightly with rapeseed oil and then pour the batter into the moulds.

Carefully lower the trays into the idli pan, cover and steam for 15 minutes. After 15 minutes, you should have delicious, fluffy idlis. To check for doneness, stick a toothpick or fork into the centre of one or two. If it comes out clean, your idlis are ready. If it comes out with a little batter stuck to it, continue steaming for a couple more minutes. Remove the trays from the steamer and let the steamed idlis sit, undisturbed, for about 2 minutes before removing them from the moulds. A small knife or spoon will help you lift the cooked idlis neatly out of the moulds.

Serve the idlis with chutneys and/or sambar. In the photograph, from top to bottom, are 40-garlic-clove chutney (see page 139), green chilli chutney (see page 142), coconut chutney (see page 143) and ginger chutney (see page 140).

(GF) (V)

I once referred to sambar as a soup on my blog and on Twitter. You wouldn't believe how many Indian cooks here in the UK and in the subcontinent quickly corrected me. Sambar is not a soup, it's sambar! While I was staying in London for the photo shoot for this book, I happened to visit a restaurant called Dosa & Chutney. They served sambar with mini idlis in a bowl and I ordered it. It was fantastic and I decided to share the idea with you here. By the way, it was served with a spoon in a bowl like a soup! Often, chopped vegetables like aubergine and okra are added to the sambar so feel free to do the same.

Sambar is the perfect accompaniment for uttapams (see page 106), and dosas (see page 115 and 116) and of course idlis (see page 108) too. Dip them in the spicy sambar and enjoy!

MINI IDLIS IN SAMBAR
SERVES 4 OR MORE AS PART OF A MULTI-COURSE MEAL

PREP TIME: 20 MINUTES, PLUS SOAKING
COOKING TIME: 1 HOUR

225g (1¼ cups) toor dhal (split pigeon pea lentils, see page 155)
1 tsp rapeseed oil
4 large tomatoes, chopped
1 tbsp finely chopped ginger
1 green chilli pepper, chopped
50g (⅓ cup) fresh or frozen peas
1 tsp ground turmeric
1 tsp red chilli powder
1 tbsp sugar
1 tsp garam masala
1 small bunch of coriander (cilantro)
1 tsp salt (or to taste)
6 mini idlis or broken larger idlis per bowl

FOR THE TARKA
60ml (¼ cup) rapeseed oil
1 tsp brown mustard seeds
1 tsp cumin seeds
A pinch of asafoetida (see page 155)
20 fresh curry leaves (see page 155)

Soak the split pigeon peas in hot water for 20 minutes. Drain and rinse, then pour them into a large saucepan. Add 1½ litres (6 cups) water and heat over high heat. As you do this, a foam will rise to the top. Skim this off until no foam remains, then reduce the heat to a simmer. Simmer for about 30 minutes until the lentils are soft.

Add the chopped tomatoes, ginger and green chilli to the pan and bring to the boil for about 3 minutes. Now, using a hand-held blender (or countertop blender), blend until smooth and creamy.

Add the rest of the ingredients and simmer for a further 15 minutes. Remove the sambar from the heat while you make your tarka.

To make the tarka, heat the oil until visibly hot in a small saucepan. Toss in the mustard seeds. They will begin to pop in the hot oil. When they do, add the cumin seeds, asafoetida and curry leaves. Fry for a further 30 seconds until the curry leaves are fragrant.

Carefully pour the tarka over the sambar. Your sambar is now ready to serve. If you are adding the mini idlis as I did in the photograph opposite, add them to the sambar and heat them through to serve.

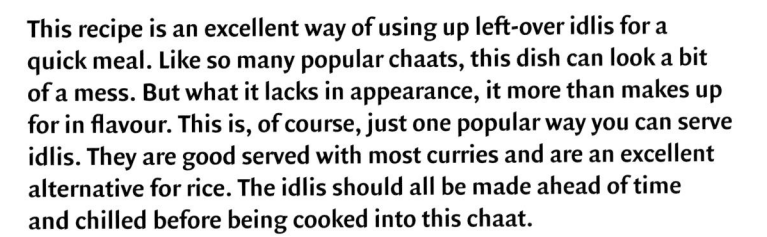

This recipe is an excellent way of using up left-over idlis for a quick meal. Like so many popular chaats, this dish can look a bit of a mess. But what it lacks in appearance, it more than makes up for in flavour. This is, of course, just one popular way you can serve idlis. They are good served with most curries and are an excellent alternative for rice. The idlis should all be made ahead of time and chilled before being cooked into this chaat.

IDLI AND KEEMA CHAAT
SERVES 4 OR MORE AS PART OF A MULTI-COURSE MEAL

PREP TIME: 10 MINUTES, PLUS MAKING THE IDLIS
COOKING TIME: 20 MINUTES

2 tbsp rapeseed oil
1 large onion, finely chopped
3 green chillies, chopped
2 tbsp mixed garlic and ginger paste (see page 7)
1 tsp chilli powder
1 tsp ground cumin
400g (14oz) minced (ground) lamb
400g (14oz) can chopped tomatoes
400g (14oz) can chickpeas (garbanzo beans), drained
10 cold idlis, broken into pieces
100ml (scant ½ cup) base curry sauce (see pages 50 or 51, optional)
1 tsp garam masala
Chaat masala (see page 155) or salt, to taste
Chutneys or pickle, to serve (optional)

FOR THE TEMPERED OIL

2 tbsp rapeseed oil
1 tsp mustard seeds
20 fresh curry leaves (see page 155)

To make the chaat, heat 2 tablespoons of oil in a large pan or wok. When visibly hot, toss in the chopped onion and chillies. Fry over medium–high heat until the onion is soft and translucent – about 5 minutes should do. Add the garlic and ginger paste and stir it all up in the oil for about 30 seconds. Stir in the chilli powder and cumin, then add the minced (ground) lamb. Brown the meat until almost cooked, then stir in the idlis and chickpeas (garbanzo beans). Stir this mixture all together and add the base curry sauce or 100ml (scant ½ cup) of water. Lower the heat while you temper the oil that will be poured over the top.

For the tempered oil, heat the oil in a small saucepan over high heat until visibly hot. Spoon in the mustard seeds. When they begin to pop, reduce the heat to medium and add the curry leaves. Let this sizzle for about 30 more seconds, then pour it on top of the chaat.

Sprinkle with the garam masala and stir it in. Season with chaat masala or salt, to taste.

Ensure the chaat is piping hot and serve on its own or with the chutney and/or pickle of your choice.

TIP: I often serve this dish with a simple onion pickle. Finely slice a red onion. Squeeze the juice of two lemons over it. Add 1 teaspoon of roasted cumin seeds and salt and sugar to taste and stir well. Allow the flavours to develop in the fridge for 30 minutes or longer.

Masala dosas are by far the most popular dosas on restaurant menus. The potato filling is delicious on its own, too. I often make some up for a quick lunch even when I don't have any dosa batter. The filling is also nice served cold as a filling for pani puris (see page 26). These dosas are perfect served with a few chutneys. Try them with my 40-garlic-clove chutney (see page 139), ginger chutney (see page 140) spicy coriander chutney (see page 141) and coconut chutney (see page 143) and/or coconut, chilli and onion chutney (see page 140). Sambar (see page 111) is also a must!

MASALA DOSA
SERVES 4

PREP TIME: 10 MINUTES
COOKING TIME: 30 MINUTES

FOR THE POTATO MASALA
2 tbsp ghee or butter
10 fresh curry leaves (see page 155)
1 tsp cumin seeds
1 onion, finely chopped
2 green chillies, finely chopped
4 large potatoes, peeled and cut into small cubes
$^1/_2$ tsp ground turmeric
3 tbsp chopped coriander (cilantro) leaves
Salt and freshly ground black pepper

FOR THE DOSAS
$^1/_2$ recipe quantity authentic batter (see page 105), or a whole batch of cheat's batter (see page 104)
$^1/_2$ tbsp rapeseed oil per dosa, for drizzling

Start by making the potato masala filling. Melt the ghee in a large wok or frying pan over medium–high heat. When melted, add the curry leaves and cumin seeds. Fry these for about 40 seconds, then add the chopped onions and chillies. Add the cubed potatoes and the turmeric and fry for a few minutes. Add just enough water to cover, then simmer the potatoes until cooked through and the water has evaporated. Mash lightly, sprinkle in the coriander (cilantro) and season to taste. Set aside while you make the dosas.

Heat a 30cm (12in) non-stick frying pan over high heat. Your pan is hot enough when a few drops of water evaporate immediately when splashed into the pan. Rub a cold, wet towel over the surface to cool it a little. Pour about 150ml ($^1/_2$ cup) of the batter into the centre of the pan. Use the back of a ladle or a flat-bottomed cup to spread the batter outwards in a circular motion until you have a thin dosa.

Don't panic if you are new to this, just do your best to spread the batter out evenly, as thinly as possible over the surface of the pan. If you mess up, it will still taste good. Remember that the thinner you spread the batter, the crispier the dosa will be.

As the underside cooks, the edges of the dosa will begin to get crispy and break away from the pan. When this happens, drizzle about $^1/_2$ tablespoon of the oil around the edges of the dosa – this will make the edges nice and crispy.

When the dosa is nicely browned on the underside, add one-quarter of the potato masala and spread down the centre or evenly over the whole surface. Roll it up or fold it in half. Keep warm while you repeat the process to make the rest of your dosas.

This is another dosa recipe I like to serve smeared with homemade tomato, onion and chilli chutney (see page 141). The thing is, dosas are delicious on their own. Make the chutney if you want, use another sauce, or just eat them with freshly chopped tomatoes, cheese and onion. You really can't go wrong.

TOMATO, CHEESE AND ONION DOSA

SERVES 4

PREP TIME: 10 MINUTES
COOKING TIME: 30 MINUTES

¹/₂ recipe quantity authentic batter (see page 105), or a whole batch of cheat's batter (see page 104)
1 recipe quantity tomato, onion and chilli chutney (see page 141)
200g (7oz) paneer (see page 155), grated
1 red onion, finely chopped
1 small bunch coriander (cilantro), finely chopped
Butter (optional)
¹/₂ tbsp rapeseed oil per dosa, for drizzling

Heat a 30cm (12in) non-stick frying pan over high heat. Your pan is hot enough when a few drops of water evaporate immediately when splashed into the pan. Rub a cold wet towel over the surface of the pan to cool it down slightly. Then, pour about 150ml (¹/₂ cup) of the batter into the centre of the pan. Using the bottom of a ladle or a flat-bottomed cup, spread the batter outwards from the centre in a circular motion. It's like drawing a spiral with the ladle or cup with small circles in the centre, becoming increasingly bigger as you spread the batter. Even if your first attempts look like a complete mess, you will still be eating well.

Once you have your dosa cooking, spread some tomato, onion and chilli chutney all over the surface. It will begin to look a lot like a pizza. Sprinkle with some grated paneer, chopped red onion and coriander (cilantro). A few pieces of soft butter on top is optional but a nice and tasty touch.

When the sides of the dosa begin to lift, drizzle a little oil around the circumference of the dosa. This will make the edges nice and crispy.

Your dosa is ready when the bottom is light brown. Roll it up and serve. Keep warm while you make the remaining dosas.

TANDOORI GRILLING AND ROASTING

If you like cooking outdoors, I've got some great recipes for you. These can all be prepared in minutes, though you will need to marinate the meats for best results. No worries if cooking outdoors isn't your thing. I have given alternative recipes so that you can cook these in the oven. In fact, in the case of smaller pieces of meat, you can even fry them on the hob. Check out my shallow-fried tandoori chicken recipe on page 15 to see how you can use a couple of pieces of charcoal to make your pan-fried meats taste as if they were cooked on a barbecue or in a tandoor.

PREPARING YOUR BARBECUE FOR DIRECT HEAT COOKING

This is the way most of us cook on the barbecue. Cooking over hot coals will get you a nice char on the exterior of your meat and/or vegetables. There is so much flavour there. You might be interested to learn that many of the dishes that are called 'tandoori' in restaurants are actually just marinated in a tandoori-style marinade and then grilled (broiled) over hot coals. Often, the tandoor oven is used just for naans and a specially made grill is set up to cook succulent chicken and lamb on skewers, as well as many vegetables.

It is a good idea to build a two-level charcoal fire. Pour the charcoal into your barbecue and move it around so two-thirds of the charcoal is on one side and the rest on the other. By doing this, you will have one side that is much hotter than the other, so you can grill (broil) over intense heat and then move cooked meat and vegetables over to the other side so that you don't overcook them.

When I barbecue in this way, I use a lot of charcoal – about two shoe boxes full – as it is very important to achieve an intense heat. Light your charcoal and let it heat up until your coals are white-hot. If you hold your hand about 5cm (2in) above the fire and it is unbearably hot, you're ready to cook.

I prefer to use flat skewers as the meat moves around less than on round skewers. You could, of course, grill (broil) your meat and veggies on a barbecue grate.

PREPARING YOUR BARBECUE FOR INDIRECT COOKING

This is the method to use for roasting. You will need a barbecue with a tight fitting lid. Fill your barbecue basin with about two shoe-boxes full of charcoal on one side, leaving the other side empty. Tuck a few fire starters into the charcoal pile and light them. Let the charcoal heat up until white-hot, then place the barbecue grill over the top. Place whatever it is you are roasting on the side with no coals and cover with the lid. If you are barbecuing in this way over an extended period of time, you will need to add a few handfuls of charcoal every half hour or so.

PREPARING YOUR HOME TANDOOR OVEN FOR COOKING

Open the bottom vent completely and place a few fire starters in the tandoor, opposite the vent. Pour in about two shoe boxes full of charcoal and light, ensuring that you strategically stack as many pieces of charcoal as you can over the flames. It is important that your charcoal is as far away from the vent as possible so that air can flow freely.

Once the fire is burning nicely, place the lid on, leaving a crack open so that air can flow from the vent to the top. Close the bottom vent so that it is only one-third open. It will need an hour or more to get up to heat. To work properly, the clay walls of the oven need to be extremely hot and the tandoor needs to be at least 230°C/450°F for cooking meat, seafood and vegetables and even hotter for naans.

If you are cooking with a tandoor for the first time, be sure to read the manual first, and cure the clay walls before cooking anything.

OVEN COOKING

Ovens vary, but I usually crank mine up to 200°C/400°F/Gas 6 and cook the meat on a wire rack near the top. To get that charred appearance and flavour, place the roasted meat under a hot grill (broiler) for a couple of minutes to finish.

Over the years, this tandoori whole roast chicken has been one of my family's favourite Sunday night dinners. It is so easy to make and tastes amazing. The recipe calls for tandoori paste or tandoori masala. In my first cookbook I featured my recipe, but a good-quality commercially available brand will work just fine. You will find them at all good Asian grocers, online and also in many supermarkets.

This is my recipe for cooking in the oven. If you prefer a smokier flavour, cook it on the barbecue using the indirect cooking method (see page 119). Cooking times may vary. You could also use smoked instead of regular paprika.

TANDOORI WHOLE CHICKEN
SERVES 4

PREP TIME: 10 MINUTES, PLUS MARINATING
COOKING TIME: 1 HOUR

2.5kg (5lb 8oz) free-range chicken, skinned
Melted butter, for basting
Juice of 1–2 limes
Salt

FOR THE MARINADE
4 tbsp Greek yoghurt
2 tbsp mixed garlic and ginger paste (see page 7)
2 tsp paprika
1 heaped tbsp tandoori paste or tandoori masala (more or less to taste)

Make the marinade by mixing together all of the marinade ingredients. Rub about a quarter of the marinade inside the chicken. Make shallow incisions into the chicken breasts, legs and thighs and truss it tightly. (If you aren't familiar with how to truss a chicken, no worries. Just tie the the legs together tightly with a piece of string. It won't win you any awards for presentation but it will help the chicken cook evenly.) Rub the remaining marinade all over the chicken, ensuring that all of the incisions are covered in marinade. Allow to marinate for 3–48 hours.

When ready to cook, pre-heat your oven to its highest setting. Once the oven is hot, place the chicken in a roasting pan and roast for 40 minutes to 1 hour, basting regularly with the melted butter and cooking juices. Your chicken is ready when the juices run clear when you prick the thigh with a knife. If using a meat thermometer, aim for 75°C/165°F.

Squeeze over the lime juice and season with salt to serve.

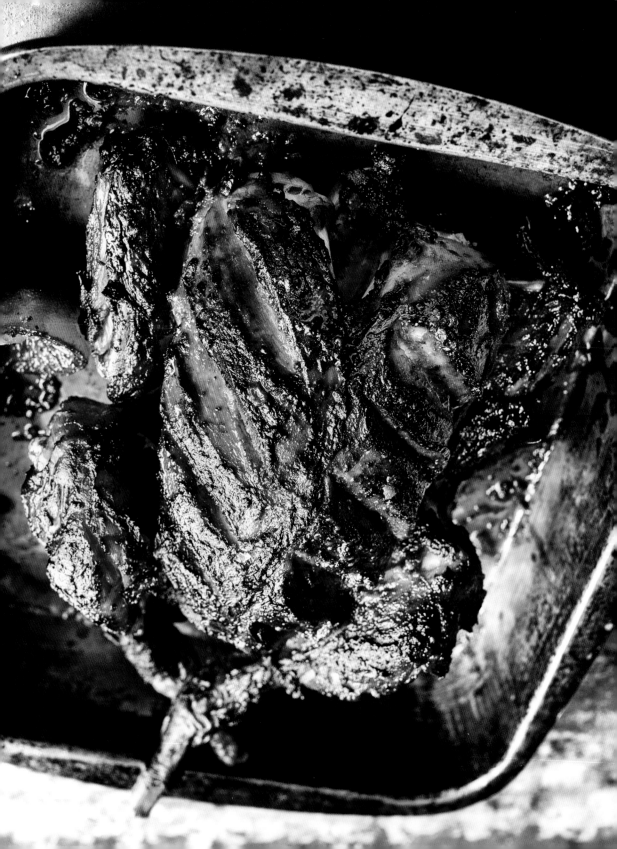

Like most of the recipes in this book, this methi chicken tikka is a mix of about ten different recipes I've seen prepared. I took the best ingredients and ideas from each and came up with this version that's a big favourite at our family barbecues.

TANDOORI METHI CHICKEN TIKKA

SERVES 4 OR MORE AS PART OF A MULTI-COURSE MEAL

PREP TIME: 15 MINUTES, PLUS MARINATING
COOKING TIME: 10 MINUTES

Juice of 2 lemons
800g (1lb 12oz) skinned chicken thighs or breasts, cut into 7.5cm (3in) pieces
3 tbsp mixed garlic and ginger paste (see page 7)
2 large bunches of fresh fenugreek (methi) leaves* (about 100g/3½oz)
3 tbsp mustard oil* or rapeseed oil
1 tbsp cumin seeds
250ml (1 cup) Greek yoghurt
5 tbsp finely chopped coriander (cilantro) leaves
1 tbsp green chilli paste
1 tbsp red chilli powder
1 tbsp garam masala
1 tbsp gram (chickpea) flour
3 tbsp cream cheese
1 tbsp rapeseed oil
50g (3½ tbsp) unsalted butter, melted
Salt
Raita and naan breads, to serve

* Fresh fenugreek is best, but see page 7 if you would like to use dried or alternative ingredients.

* If using mustard oil, heat it up until bubbles form, then let it cool before using.

Squeeze the lemon juice over the chicken and rub in 1 tablespoon of the garlic and ginger paste. Set aside while you make the marinade.

Chop up your fresh fenugreek leaves and thin stalks finely. Blanch in a pot of boiling water for about 30 seconds. Drain and squeeze out the excess moisture and set aside to cool slightly. Using a food processor or blender, blend the fenugreek leaves until you have a smooth purée. You may need to add a little fresh water to help it blend. Set aside.

Now heat the oil in a large frying pan over medium–high heat until visibly hot. If using mustard oil, it will give off a strong, nutty aroma. Throw in the cumin seeds. When they begin to pop, add the fenugreek purée you prepared. Stir it into the oil and fry for about 30 seconds, then set aside to cool.

Put the yoghurt in a large bowl and whisk it until smooth. Add the rest of the garlic and ginger paste, the coriander (cilantro), chilli paste, red chilli powder, garam masala, gram flour, cream cheese and rapeseed oil. Work this together with your hands until all of the ingredients become a smooth emulsion. Add the cooled fenugreek mixture to this and continue to work it into a smooth marinade.

Cover the chicken and marinate for 3–24 hours. When ready to cook, light about two shoe boxes full of charcoal on your barbecue. When the charcoal is white hot, you're ready to cook.

Skewer your chicken, leaving a small space between each piece, and grill (broil) on one side until nicely charred. Flip the skewers over and continue grilling (broiling) until cooked through – it will take about 10 minutes. Just before the meat is cooked, baste it with the melted butter. Remove to a warm plate and let rest for about 5 minutes before serving. Check the seasoning and serve with your favourite raita and naans.

You can also roast the chicken in the oven at 200°C/400°F/ Gas 6 until cooked through. Once cooked, placing the meat under a grill (broiler) will give a nice charred finish.

Minced (ground) chicken doesn't normally have a lot of fat in it. That could be seen as a good thing, but when formed into seekh kebabs the meat needs a bit of help. That's why I suggest the added butter. Most of it goes right into the fire but what remains helps make these kebabs as juicy as those made with red meat.

I originally developed this recipe for game birds. Every winter, our hunting neighbours bring around their kill of pheasants, grouse and other game birds. The fresh game meat tastes fantastic in this recipe but chicken is, of course, a lot easier to come by and is much more common at restaurants. Although I have given skewer cooking instructions here, you could also form the meat into patties or fry these kebabs in a little oil. When I do this, I leave the egg out as it is only used as a binder to help the meat stay on the skewer. You can see these skewered kebabs on the bottom right of the Contents page (see page 3).

CHICKEN SEEKH KEBABS
SERVES 4

PREP TIME: 15 MINUTES
COOKING TIME: 15 MINUTES

500g (1lb 2oz) minced (ground) chicken
1 onion, finely chopped
1 beaten egg (for skewer cooking only)
2 green chillies, finely chopped
1 tsp ground cumin
1 tsp ground coriander
2 tbsp dried chilli (hot pepper) flakes
1/2 tsp ground turmeric
1 tsp salt (more or less to taste)
1 tsp dried thyme
3 tbsp butter, softened, plus more to baste

Prepare your barbecue for direct heat cooking (see page 119).

Mix all the ingredients together well. Divide the mixture into four equal-sized balls and spear each ball onto its own skewer. Take the first skewer and squeeze the meat tightly around the skewer so that it stretches out to form a sausage shape. Continue squeezing and turning the skewer until the sausage becomes long and tightly wrapped on the skewer. It shouldn't move when shaken lightly. This can take a little time. You want the meat to be tightly pressed onto the skewer so that it doesn't fall off when cooking. Repeat with the remaining 3 skewers.

Place the skewers over your fire and cook, without turning, until the underside is nicely charred. Flip over to continue cooking on the other side until the meat is cooked through. Baste each kebab with a little more butter before serving. Although delicious on their own, it's hard to beat these succulent chicken kebabs wrapped up into hot naans with a little salad and your sauces of choice.

You've got to love a good shawarma kebab! Perfectly marinated pieces of meat that are nice and crisp on the exterior and juicy and tender in the centre. I'm getting hungry just writing about it. At UK takeaways, beef, chicken and lamb are marinated and then placed on a rotating spit. The meat is shaved off with a large electric knife and then served in fresh naans topped with salad, hot sauce and/or yoghurt dressing.

I don't have a large spit, nor the need to cook as much meat as takeaways do, so I decided to downsize this recipe a bit. You will need metal skewers and a good barbecue for best results. I like to add vegetables like red onions and peppers (bell peppers) to the skewers that are delicious served with the marinated, grilled (broiled) meat.

SHAWARMA KEBABS

SERVES 4–6

PREP TIME: 15 MINUTES, PLUS FREEZING AND MARINATING
COOKING TIME: 15 MINUTES

6 large chicken breasts
Red onion, chillies and peppers (bell peppers), chopped
Naans, buns or tortillas, to serve
Sauces of your choice, to serve

FOR THE MARINADE
5 tbsp olive oil
2 tbsp mixed garlic and ginger paste (see page 7)
1 tbsp ground cumin
1 tbsp ground coriander
1 tsp ground allspice
½ tsp ground turmeric
½ tsp ground cinnamon
1 tbsp paprika
Salt and freshly ground black pepper

Place the chicken breasts in the freezer for 30 minutes – this will help you slice them. Remove from the freezer and slice into thin disks.

Place all the marinade ingredients in a bowl and mix well. Add your chicken discs to the marinade and ensure it is all nicely coated. Marinate for 30 minutes or up to 24 hours.

When ready to cook, light your charcoal using the direct cooking method (see page 119) and wait until white hot.

In the meantime, skewer the marinated chicken discs on the metal skewers so that they are pressed tightly together. I like to include some red onions, chillies and peppers (bell peppers) for colour. See the photo opposite.

Place the skewers over the heat and rotate often until charred on the outside and cooked through – about 15 minutes. Remove the meat and chop into small pieces. Serve on its own or wrapped in fresh naans, buns or tortillas with your sauces of choice.

I love the deep green colour of these kebabs and the flavour is out of this world. Just look at the photograph on page 124! Be sure to keep some of the marinade aside to brush over the chicken pieces just before they're cooked through. You can also cook these on a grill (broiler) if the barbecue isn't set up or even in the oven if you wish. See the note below.

MEAN AND GREEN CHICKEN TIKKA KEBABS

SERVES 4 OR MORE AS PART OF A MULTI-COURSE MEAL

PREP TIME: 15 MINUTES, PLUS MARINATING
COOKING TIME: 20 MINUTES

4 tbsp rapeseed oil
1 onion, finely chopped
8 green chillies, finely chopped (feel free to use less if you don't like it very hot)
1 tbsp ground cumin
$\frac{1}{2}$ tsp ground turmeric
3 large handfuls of baby spinach leaves
3 tbsp mixed garlic and ginger paste (see page 7)
Juice of 2 lemons
10 cashews
100g (7 tbsp) butter
15 mint leaves
1 large bunch of coriander (cilantro)
3 tbsp thick Greek yoghurt
1 tbsp garam masala (or more or less to taste)
800g (1lb 12oz) skinless chicken breasts, cut into bite-sized pieces
Salt and freshly ground black pepper

In a large pan, heat the oil over medium–high heat. When visibly hot, tip in your chopped onion and green chillies and sizzle until the onion is translucent and soft. Now add the cumin and turmeric and stir it all up. Add the spinach, garlic and ginger and stir it all into the onion. As you cook, the spinach will wilt. Remove this marinade from the heat and allow to cool for a few minutes.

In a blender or food processor, blend the spinach and onion mixture with the lemon juice, cashews, butter, mint and coriander (cilantro). You might need to add a drop of water to do this. Whisk this mixture in a bowl with the yoghurt until smooth and creamy and check for seasoning, adding the garam masala and salt and pepper to taste.

Remove about 250ml (1 cup) of the marinade and set aside for later. Pour the remaining marinade over the chicken pieces and allow to marinate for at least 3 and up to 48 hours.

When ready to cook, light your charcoal using the direct cooking method (see page 119). Skewer the chicken pieces (tikka), leaving a small space between each piece and place over the hot coals. Allow the meat to cook and get a good char on the underside before turning. Flip the skewers over and cook through. You can rotate the skewers from time to time for more even cooking.

Just before serving, baste with the marinade you set aside earlier.

 You can also roast the chicken in the oven at 200°C/400°F/ Gas 6 until cooked through. Once cooked, placing the meat under a grill (broiler) will give a nice charred finish.

The marinade used in this recipe is good on any meat, not just lamb. The first time I made this I took it camping with my family. The meat had already been marinating for about 48 hours but when we got there and I finally got my disaster of a tent put up, I was in no mood to start cooking. So we cooked the following evening, and I have to say that extra 24 hours of marinating really worked a treat! There is a lot of talk these days that meat doesn't benefit from excessively long marinating times. All I know is that meal was amazing and one we all still talk about.

TANDOORI LAMB TIKKA
SERVES 4 OR MORE AS PART OF A MULTI-COURSE MEAL

PREP TIME: 15 MINUTES, PLUS MARINATING
COOKING TIME: 20 MINUTES

4 tbsp mixed garlic and ginger paste (see page 7)
2 tbsp green chilli paste
800g (1lb 12oz) lamb leg meat, trimmed of fat and cut into cubes
½ tsp salt (or to taste)
Juice of 2 limes
1 tbsp garam masala
1 tsp red chilli power
1 tbsp ground cumin
1 tsp ground coriander
1 tsp dried fenugreek (methi) leaves
1 tsp mustard oil
1 tsp English mustard
3 tbsp plain yoghurt
1 tbsp mint sauce
Salad, raita and naan breads, to serve

Rub the garlic and ginger and green chilli pastes into the meat and set aside for about 20 minutes.

To make the marinade, blend the rest of the ingredients together until very smooth. Cover the lamb cubes with the marinade and allow to marinate for 3–72 hours. The longer the better.

When ready to cook, remove the meat from the marinade. Skewer the meat, leaving a little space between each piece so that it cooks evenly and the outside crisps right up. Heat your coals until very hot and white.

Grill (broil) the meat, turning regularly, for about 10 minutes, or until it is crisp and nicely browned on the outside. Don't worry too much about this. I am a rare-meat fan but have over-cooked the lamb on occasion and it still comes out beautifully even when well done.

Serve as it is with a nice green salad and raita, or wrap it up in a homemade naan. The meat can also be used in any lamb curry.

Piri piri dishes are now popular all over the world. Originally a Portuguese recipe that is believed to have been first made in the former Portuguese colony of Mozambique, piri piri was introduced to the native population of Goa during the Portuguese occupation. The sauce was made from red sweet peppers (bell peppers), paprika and red piri piri chillies, but many other varieties are used now.

It is believed that the red piri piri sauce was the inspiration behind chicken cafreal, which is made with similar ingredients but with additional green chillies, coriander (cilantro) and mint to make a green sauce. So it's little wonder that this spicy Portuguese dish that was loved by the Goan population is now finding its way on to many Indian restaurant menus. Double the sauce recipe if you like a lot of sauce.

PIRI PIRI CHICKEN

SERVES 4 OR MORE AS PART OF A MULTI-COURSE MEAL

PREP TIME: 15 MINUTES, PLUS MARINATING AND CHILLING
COOKING TIME: 1–1¼ HOURS

5 tbsp rapeseed oil
½ onion, finely chopped
1 red pepper (bell pepper), roughly chopped
8 garlic cloves, peeled
4 green or red chillies, roughly chopped
2 tbsp smoked or normal paprika
1 tbsp cayenne pepper (more or less to taste)
1 tsp freshly ground black pepper
1 tbsp dried chilli (hot pepper) flakes
3 tbsp lemon juice
70ml (generous ¼ cup) white wine vinegar
1.5kg (3lb 5oz) chicken thighs, bone-in and skin left on
Salt and freshly ground black pepper
Lime slices, to serve

Heat the oil in a saucepan over medium–high heat and add the onion and pepper (bell pepper). Fry until the onion is translucent and soft, then add the garlic and chillies. Fry for a further minute or so, then add 1 tablespoon of the paprika, the cayenne chilli powder, black pepper and chilli (hot pepper) flakes and season with salt.

Add the lemon juice and vinegar and simmer for about 5 minutes. Allow to cool slightly, then blend until very smooth and place this marinade in the fridge for about 30 minutes.

When ready to prepare your chicken, season the thighs generously with salt and pepper and the remaining paprika and pour over half of the piri piri sauce. Stir it all up so that the chicken is nicely coated and marinate in the fridge for no more than 3 hours.

When ready to cook, heat your oven to its highest temperature. Remove as much of the marinade as you can and stir it into the marinade you set aside. Place the chicken in a roasting tray and cook for 40 minutes–1 hour until the chicken is crisp and cooked through.

Transfer the chicken to a warm serving plate, then whisk the retained marinade into the cooking juices in the tray. Bring to a rolling simmer. You can either pour this over the chicken or serve it like a gravy at the table. Serve the chicken drizzled with the sauce and topped with slices of lime. I love this dish cooked using the indirect cooking method (see page 119) on the barbecue.

This is one you are very unlikely to find at a curry house but it was too good to leave out of the book. I've been making beer can chicken for many years and this Indian-inspired version is one of my current favourites. You could also easily make this in a conventional oven. See my tip below.

TANDOORI BEER CAN CHICKEN

SERVES 4

PREP TIME: 10 MINUTES, PLUS MARINATING
COOKING TIME: 1–1½ HOURS

100ml (scant ½ cup) rapeseed oil
440ml (15fl oz) can of your favourite beer or lager
900g (2lb) whole chicken

FOR THE MARINADE
2 tbsp mixed garlic and ginger paste (see page 7)
1 tbsp paprika
1 tsp ground cumin
1 tsp dried oregano
½ tsp red chilli powder
1 tsp ground turmeric
1 small bunch of coriander (cilantro), blended with a little water
Salt and freshly ground black pepper

Blend all the marinade ingredients into a paste or pound them using a pestle and mortar. Slowly drizzle the rapeseed oil into the paste, whisking continuously until you have a smooth emulsion. Cover the chicken inside and out with the marinade and allow to marinate for 8 hours or overnight. I carefully rub about half of the marinade under the skin but don't worry if you can't be bothered.

When ready to cook, set up your barbecue for indirect cooking (see page 119). Drink half the can of beer or lager and add 1 teaspoon of marinade from the chicken dish to it. The beer might foam up when you add the marinade but that isn't a problem.

When your barbecue is good and hot you're ready to cook. If you have a thermometer, aim for a cooking temperature of 190–200°C/ 375–400°F. Place the chicken, standing on the beer can directly on the barbecue on the side with no coals. Cover and cook for about 1–1¼ hours until the chicken is cooked through and the juices run clear when stuck with a knife in the thigh. You can't be too careful with chicken so if you have a meat thermometer, check that your chicken is 82°C/180°F.

When cooked through, transfer to a serving plate and cover with foil to sit for about 10 minutes before serving.

TIP: You can also cook the chicken in the oven. Preheat the oven to 230°C/450°F/Gas 8. Place the chicken on a half-full beer can in a roasting tray and roast for 20 minutes. Reduce the heat to 200°C/ 400°F/Gas 6 and continue to roast until cooked through and the juices run clear, about another 30 minutes. Check for seasoning and add salt to taste. Let the chicken rest for about 10 minutes before carving.

 GF

Duck legs are usually a lot cheaper than purchasing a whole duck, and the meat from the legs is the tastiest part of the bird. Depending on how hungry you are, you might want to double this recipe. It's perfect served with a simple green salad and/or turmeric tomatoes (see page 149), as seen in the top-right of the photograph, opposite.

SLOW-ROAST GARAM MASALA DUCK LEGS

SERVES 6

PREP TIME: 5 MINUTES, PLUS RESTING
COOKING TIME: 3 HOURS

6 duck legs
1–2 tbsp garam masala
Salt and freshly ground black
  pepper

Sprinkle the duck legs all over with the garam masala and salt and pepper to taste. Set aside.

Pre-heat your oven to 170°C/325°F/Gas 3. Prick each leg about ten times with a sharp knife, being careful just to prick the skin and not the meat. Place them on a baking tray.

Place the duck legs in the oven and roast for 30 minutes. Then remove the legs and make ten more holes in each. This helps the fat escape and will make the skin crispier. Repeat every 30 minutes for 2 hours.

After 2 hours, increase the oven temperature to its hottest setting and roast for another 30 minutes. The duck legs should now be ready. Take them out of the oven and allow to rest for 20 minutes. The skin will become crispier as it rests.

Cut the duck into small pieces with a sharp knife or simply pick up the legs and dig in.

The flavour and aroma of smoky lamb chops covered in lemon and anchovy butter is to die for. My friend, Palash Mitra, Head Chef at Gymkhana in London, showed me this recipe a few years back and I've made it many times since. It's definitely worth a try! I like to serve these with turmeric tomatoes (see page 149).

LAMB CHOPS ᴡɪᴛʜ LEMON ANCHOVY BUTTER
SERVES 4 OR MORE AS PART OF A MULTI-COURSE MEAL

PREP TIME: 15 MINUTES, PLUS MARINATING
COOKING TIME: 8 MINUTES

FOR THE LEMON ANCHOVY BUTTER
40g (3 tbsp) unsalted butter
8–10 anchovy fillets, crushed to a paste
Juice of 1 lemon

FOR THE LAMB CHOPS
8 lamb chops on the bone
2 tbsp mixed garlic and ginger paste (see page 7)
1 tsp salt
1 tsp amchoor (dried mango powder, see page 155)
2 tbsp mustard oil
2 tbsp crème fraîche
2 tsp white wine vinegar
2 green chillies, deseeded and finely chopped
1 large handful coriander (cilantro) stalks, finely chopped
a small handful of mint leaves, finely chopped
1 tsp garam masala
1 tsp sugar
1 tsp chilli powder
A few drops of rosewater
A few drops of Himalayan screwpine water (available online and in Asian food shops, optional)

Place the butter in a bowl and leave in a warm place for about 10 minutes. Then whisk it until smooth. Add the anchovies and lemon juice and fold it all together. Keep chilled.

Rub the garlic and ginger paste and salt into the lamb chops and leave for 10 minutes.

Mix all the remaining ingredients together in a non-metallic bowl. Add the lamb chops to the bowl and rub the marinade into the meat well. Leave for 30 minutes or up to 48 hours.

When ready to cook, fire up your barbecue using the direct grilling method (see page 119) and place the lamb chops on the grill (broiler). Grill (broil) for about 8 minutes, turning only once, or until the exterior is crispy and blackened and medium–rare in the centre. (Alternatively, you could sear them in a hot frying pan with a little oil. About 2 minutes per side should get them nicely charred. Then turn regularly until cooked to your preferred doneness.)

Let rest on a warmed plate for a few minutes, then place the chargrilled lamb chops on warm plates, top with the lemon anchovy butter and serve.

Many curry houses serve lamb raan but don't expect to simply walk in and order. Most restaurants will ask for three days' notice and a deposit if you want to treat your family and/or friends to a leg of lamb raan. The long marination time is part of the reason for this. To be honest, I cheated once and only marinated the meat for 3 hours with outstanding results.

LAMB RAAN

SERVES 6 OR MORE AS PART OF A MULTI-COURSE MEAL

**PREP TIME: 15 MINUTES,
PLUS MARINATING
COOKING TIME: 3 HOURS**

1 leg of lamb, surface fat
  removed (ask your butcher
  to do this)
2 bulbs of garlic
3cm (1¼in) piece of ginger
3 onions, finely sliced and fried
  in oil until nicely browned
1 tsp chilli powder (more or less
  to taste)
1 tbsp tandoori masala
500ml (2 cups) Greek yoghurt
2 red onions, cut into large
  chunks
2 bay leaves
1 cinnamon stick
200ml (¾ cup) meat stock
  (optional)
Oil, for greasing
1 tsp chaat masala (see page 155)
Juice of 1–2 limes
Salt and freshly ground black
  pepper

Pierce the leg of lamb all over with a sharp knife. Slice two garlic cloves into thin slivers, insert the slivers into the holes in the lamb.

To make the marinade, put the rest of the garlic, the ginger, fried onions, chilli powder and tandoori masala and half the yoghurt in a blender and blend until smooth. Stir this into the remaining yoghurt.

To marinate, roll out a large piece of cling film (plastic wrap) that will wrap around the leg of lamb several times. Place the leg of lamb on the cling film and pour the marinade all over it. Rub the marinade into the flesh and press it into the holes with the garlic. Wrap it up tightly in the cling film and place in the fridge for 2–3 days.

When ready to cook, preheat your oven to 180°C/350°F/Gas 4. Rub all of the marinade off of the meat and tap it dry with a paper towel. Retain the marinade to make a sauce. Place the red onions at the bottom of a greased metal roasting pan and secure the leg of lamb on top. Toss the bay leaves and cinnamon stick into the pan, sprinkle with black pepper and cover it all tightly with foil.

Place the lamb in the oven and cook for 2½ hours. The meat should be fall-off-the-bone tender. Remove the meat from the pan and deglaze the pan with the meat stock or 200ml (¾ cup) water. Strain the cooking juices into a saucepan and simmer until it is quite thick – not sauce consistency, but close. Stir in 4–5 tablespoons of the reserved marinade, 1 tablespoon at a time. Don't add all at once or it will curdle. Check for seasoning and keep warm.

Sprinkle the lamb with the chaat masala and black pepper and place the leg back into the deglazed roasting tray. To finish, heat your oven to its highest temperature and place the lamb back in the oven until nicely charred (ovens vary, so this last step may not be necessary if your lamb already has a good colour). Squeeze the lime juice over the lamb and slice at the table. Serve with the sauce.

TIP: You can also cut the lamb into small pieces to enjoy wrapped in naans with a few of your favourite salads, chutneys and raitas.

ACCOMPANIMENTS

SPICY CORIANDER CHUTNEY/RAITA

MAKES: 250ML (1 CUP)

This super-easy chutney is superb drizzled over meat, vegetables, breads, rice and dosas. You can easily make it into a delicious raita by whisking in about 250ml (1 cup) plain yoghurt. I serve the raita version often with kebabs and biryanis.

PREP TIME: 5 MINUTES

1 tsp roasted cumin seeds
1 large bunch of coriander (cilantro)
3 green chillies (more or less to taste)
2 garlic cloves
Juice of 1 lemon
Salt

Blend all the ingredients until you have a smooth chutney. You might need to add a drop of water to help everything blend. That's it... your work is done.

TIP: If you are adding the yoghurt to make this a raita, I recommend blending everything as above, and then just stirring in the yoghurt rather than adding it to the blender. You will get a better, thicker, result.

40-GARLIC-CLOVE CHUTNEY

MAKES 200ML (¾ CUP)

Like garlic? You're going to love this garlic chutney! I had a basic recipe for garlic chutney but I decided to go all out and add a lot more garlic – and it worked. I promise you, if you like garlic and spice you've got to make this. I serve it with dosas and idlis, but there really is no limit as to what you can dip into it. French bread, veggies, steak... you name it, it works.

PREP TIME: 15 MINUTES
COOKING TIME: 5 MINUTES

4 tbsp rapeseed oil
40 garlic cloves, lightly crushed
10 dried Kashmiri chillies, deseeded if you want a milder chutney
1 tsp tamarind concentrate
1 tsp black mustard seeds
10 fresh or frozen curry leaves (see page 155)
Salt

Heat 2 tablespoons of the oil in a frying pan over medium–high heat. When hot, add the garlic cloves and chillies. Fry until the garlic is soft and lightly browned. Frying the garlic helps mellow it so you don't get that burning flavour of raw garlic, but be careful not to burn it or it will become bitter.

Blend the garlic, chillies and tamarind concentrate with just enough water to form a thick paste, then transfer to a serving dish. Taste this and stir in salt to taste.

Now heat up the remaining oil in a frying pan over medium–high heat. When hot, add the mustard seeds. When the seeds begin to pop, add the curry leaves and fry for another 30 seconds. Pour this oil mixture over the garlic chutney and serve. Garlic chutney can be eaten hot or cold.

GINGER CHUTNEY

MAKES 200ML (¾ CUP)

Whenever I make dosas, uttapams or idlis, this ginger chutney has to be on the table. It has such a unique flavour that I have grown to love. Actually, I took the idea from my grandparents' family cookbook and then gave it an Indian touch. I promise you, though, it is good enough to be served at any south Indian restaurant.

PREP TIME: 15 MINUTES
COOKING TIME: 10 MINUTES

4 tbsp rapeseed oil
10 dried red Kashmiri chillies
1 tbsp white split urad dhal lentils (see page 155)
1 tbsp channa dhal lentils (see page 155)
10cm (4in) piece of ginger,
　　peeled and roughly chopped
1 tsp tamarind concentrate
2 tsp sugar
1 tsp salt
1 tsp black mustard seeds
10 fresh or frozen curry leaves (see page 155)

Heat 2 tablespoons of the oil in a frying pan over medium–high heat. When hot, add the chillies, urad dhal and channa dhal. Fry until the dhal is lightly browned, then pour into a blender or small food processor.

Tip the chopped ginger into the pan and fry until lightly browned and fragrant.

Add the ginger to the blender, along with the tamarind concentrate, sugar and salt, and blend with just enough water to make a thick paste. Spoon this into a serving dish.

Pour the rest of the oil into a clean frying pan set over high heat. When it is hot, pour in the mustard seeds. When these begin to pop, add the curry leaves. Fry for a further 30 seconds and then pour it all over the chutney and serve. Ginger chutney can be served hot or cold.

COCONUT, CHILLI AND ONION SAMBOL

MAKES 500ML (2 CUPS)

If you're anything like me, cutting into a coconut and attempting to get all the meat out seems a bit too much of a chore. I do it when I'm planning a really special dinner, but have found the shredded coconut found in the freezer section of many Asian shops and larger supermarkets is a worthy second best. If using frozen coconut, be sure to let it thaw before making this sambol. It is the perfect accompaniment for dosas, idlis and uttapams.

PREP TIME: 20 MINUTES

3 red chilli peppers
Salt
1 grated coconut (or equivalent of
　　frozen grated coconut)
1 red onion, finely chopped
Juice of 1–2 limes

Using a pestle and mortar or a grinding stone, if you have one, start by grinding the chilli, salt and a splash of water to a paste. Add the coconut flesh and onion and keep grinding until you have a chunky, thick paste. Add lime juice to taste and serve. If all that grinding is going to stop you from making this, use a blender or food processor.

(GF) (V)
CORIANDER, COCONUT AND CHILLI CHUTNEY

MAKES 200ML (¾ CUP)

This chutney is a good all-rounder. It is great served with everything from pakoras to idlis, pappadams and, of course, dosas.

PREP TIME: 15 MINUTES
COOKING TIME: 5 MINUTES

1 large bunch of coriander (cilantro)
1½ tbsp mixed garlic and ginger paste (see page 7)
1 tsp roasted cumin seeds
3 green chillies
70g (2½oz) grated fresh coconut or frozen coconut flesh (plus a little of the coconut water)
2 tbsp coconut amino (see page 155) or soy sauce
Juice of 1–2 limes
3 tbsp rapeseed oil
1 tsp brown mustard seeds
10 fresh or frozen curry leaves (see page 155)

Put the coriander (cilantro), garlic and ginger paste, cumin seeds, chillies, grated coconut, coconut amino and lime juice, to taste, in a blender and blend until smooth and thick with a drizzle of the retained coconut water just to help it blend. (If you are using frozen coconut and don't have any water, a splash of tap water will be fine). This can be stored in the fridge, covered, overnight.

When ready to serve, pour the rapeseed oil into a small frying pan set over medium–high heat. When the oil is visibly hot, add the mustard seeds. When the seeds begin to pop, stir in the curry leaves and fry for about 20 seconds.

Put the prepared chutney in a serving bowl and pour the oil mixture over the top to serve.

(GF) (V)
TOMATO, ONION AND CHILLI CHUTNEY

MAKES 500ML (2 CUPS)

This one may be simple but the flavours all work so well together. You can serve it however you see fit. It's a good one to have on hand to be eaten with anything from meat to idlis. I like to use it just like a pizza sauce on dosas, like the tomato, paneer and onion dosas (see page 116). It is also nice served as a side sauce.

PREP TIME: 5 MINUTES, PLUS SOAKING
COOKING TIME: 10 MINUTES

8 (more or less) dried Kashmiri chillies
2 tbsp rapeseed oil
1 tsp white split urad dhal lentils (see page 155)
1 small onion, finely chopped
8 garlic cloves
250g (9oz) canned chopped tomatoes or chopped fresh tomatoes
Salt

Soak the chillies in water for about 30 minutes. Remove the chillies from the water and tear in half. Remove the seeds if you don't want your chutney to be really spicy.

In a frying pan, temper the urad dhal in the oil over medium–high heat for about 30 seconds, then add the chopped onion. When the onion becomes soft and translucent, add the garlic cloves and fry for a further 2 minutes, or until the garlic cloves are just beginning to turn light brown. Transfer all of this to a spice grinder with the tomatoes and grind until smooth.

Season with salt to taste and serve.

TOMATO SALSA

MAKES ABOUT 500ML (2 CUPS)

I've been making this salsa since I was in school. Back then it was served as an accompaniment for Mexican dishes. Actually, it still is because after Indian food, Mexican is what I make most at home.

A few years back, I was at a food festival in Leeds where one of the vendors was serving seekh kebab and chicken tikka wraps. They had a lot of delicious sauces to top the wraps with and one was exactly like this salsa. So many of the ingredients used in Mexican food and the food of the Indian subcontinent are similar, but I loved how this authentic Mexican salsa had not only jumped continents once to become an authentic Pakistani chutney, but had then ended up being served at a food stall in the UK. The beer, by the way, isn't used in the Pakistani version, but I like it.

PREP TIME: 10 MINUTES

400g (14oz) can chopped tomatoes
1 small onion, roughly chopped
3 garlic cloves, smashed
4 green chilli peppers, chopped (more or less to taste)
1 small bunch of coriander (cilantro), chopped
Juice of 1–2 limes
50ml (3½ tbsp) beer (you can drink the rest)
Salt

Place all the ingredients in a blender and blend until the tomato chutney is smooth but still has a bit of texture. Check for seasoning and serve. I find that a good dose of salt really brings out the flavours.

That's it! Believe me, this simple tomato chutney can make a good meal great!

GREEN CHILLI CHUTNEY

MAKES 400ML (1¾ CUPS)

This spicy chutney is only for those who can take the heat. Like so many of the chutneys I have for you in this book, you can make this well ahead of time and serve it with whatever you think will taste good with fiery hot chopped chillies.

PREP TIME: 10 MINUTES
COOKING TIME: 10 MINUTES

3 tbsp rapeseed oil
40 green chillies
20 garlic cloves
1 tbsp cumin seeds
35g (½ cup) desiccated (dried shredded) coconut
1 tsp salt
1 tsp sugar
1 small bunch of coriander (cilantro) leaves
Juice of 2 limes
1 tbsp tamarind paste (optional)

FOR THE TARKA
3 tbsp rapeseed oil
1 tsp mustard seeds
1 tsp cumin seeds
½ tsp asafoetida (see page 155)
2 garlic cloves, smashed

Heat the oil and fry the chillies over medium–high heat. Add the garlic, desiccated coconut and cumin seeds and stir to combine. Fry for a couple of minutes until the peppers and garlic are turning soft. Transfer to a food processor and add the salt, sugar and coriander (cilantro) and pulse to a chunky paste. Set aside.

Now heat the remaining oil in a small frying pan over a high heat. When visibly hot, stir in the mustard seeds. When they begin to pop, stir in the cumin seeds, asafoetida and smashed garlic. Sizzle for 30 seconds, then pour the flavoured oil over the chutney. Stir in the lime juice. For a bit more zing, stir in the tamarind paste, too, then serve.

COCONUT CHUTNEY

MAKES 500ML (2 CUPS)

I always make a chutney like this when I serve dosas, idlis and/or uttapams. Coconut chutney is often made with fresh coconut but good-quality desiccated coconut or coconut flakes are a good substitute.

PREP TIME: 5 MINUTES
COOKING TIME: 5 MINUTES

2 tbsp rapeseed oil
1 tbsp white split urad dhal (see page 155)
2 tbsp split chana dhal (see page 155)
200g (1 cup) organic desiccated (dried shredded) coconut, soaked in 175ml ($^3/_4$ cup) water for 20 minutes
$^1/_2$ –1 tsp tamarind concentrate

FOR THE TARKA

1 tsp black mustard seeds
$^1/_4$ tsp asafoetida (see page 155)
3 – 4 dried red chillies torn into three pieces each
20 fresh or frozen curry leaves (see page 155)
Salt

Over medium–high heat, fry the urad dhal and chana dhal in about 2 tablespoons of the oil until fragrant and starting to brown, about 2 minutes.

Pour this into a spice grinder or pestle and mortar and add the soaked coconut and soaking water with the tamarind concentrate. Grind with about 125ml ($^1/_2$ cup) water until you have a paste. You can add a little more water if necessary. Set aside

Now heat the remaining oil over high heat in a small pan. Add the mustard seeds. When they begin to pop, stir in the asafoetida, red chillies and curry leaves. If you don't like spicy heat, remove the seeds from the dried chillies. Fry for about 30–60 seconds to season the oil and then pour it over coconut mixture.

Stir well and add salt to taste. This is a runny chutney so stir in a little more water or until the chutney is like a thick soup.

HOMEMADE ROASTED HOT PEPPER SAUCE

MAKES 550ML (2½ CUPS)

I must make a batch of this sauce every two weeks. You could use any type of chilli you want to, not just the suggested long red chillies. Feel free to experiment with different flavours and heat. Use a variety of chillies if you like. This will safely keep in the fridge for a couple of months.

PREP TIME: 10 MINUTES
COOKING TIME: 30 MINUTES

30 long red chillies, about 450g/1lb (but no need to get your scales out!)
2 tbsp rapeseed oil
$^1/_2$ onion, roughly chopped
5 garlic cloves, roughly chopped
1 tsp ground cumin
70ml (4$^1/_2$ tbsp) white wine vinegar
125ml ($^1/_2$ cup) water
Juice of 1 lemon
1 tsp sea salt flakes (or to taste)

Pre-heat your oven to 200ºC/400ºF/Gas 6.

Split all the chillies down the middle and remove the stems. Put on a baking tray and roast the chillies for about 25 minutes, or until they are slightly blackened and blistering.

While the chillies are roasting, heat the oil in a frying pan over medium–high heat and sauté the onion for about 5 minutes until soft and translucent. Add the chopped garlic and fry for a further 1 minute.

When your chillies are ready, place all the ingredients in a blender and blend until very smooth. Check for seasoning and add more salt if needed. Store in a sterilized jar with a tight-fitting lid in the fridge and use whenever you want a spice hit.

CHIP SHOP CURRY SAUCE

SERVES 2–4

Just after my first cookbook was published, I was asked onto the *Chris Evans Breakfast Show* on BBC Radio 2 to explain how to make chip shop curry sauce. Luckily, I had a good recipe for the sauce, as it wasn't in my book. After that show, I had so many people asking me for the recipe so here it is!

PREP TIME: 10 MINUTES
COOKING TIME: 20 MINUTES

2 tbsp rapeseed oil
2 onions, finely chopped
1 green apple, cored, peeled and finely chopped
2 tbsp raisins (plus more at the end if you like raisins in your sauce)
1 tbsp curry powder (or more to taste)
1 tbsp concentrated tomato purée (condensed tomato paste)
2 tbsp plain (all-purpose) flour (optional)
250ml (1 cup) base curry sauce (see pages 50 or 51) (optional)
Juice of 1 lemon
Salt and freshly ground black pepper

Heat the oil in a saucepan over medium–high heat and fry the onions and apple until soft. Stir in the raisins, curry powder and tomato paste. Add the flour, if using, to make a thicker sauce, and stir well to combine with the other ingredients. Pour in the base sauce, if using, or an equal amount of water, and simmer for about 5–10 minutes until you are happy with the consistency.

Blend well with a hand-blender or countertop blender and season with salt and pepper to taste. Check for seasoning, adding more curry powder if you like, and squeeze in the lemon juice. Stir in another 1–2 tablespoons of raisins to finish, if you like.

GREEN PANI

MAKES 700ML (3 CUPS)

Green pani (green water) is delicious poured into pani puris (see page 26). It can be made in minutes, though leaving it in the fridge for a couple of hours before serving will allow the flavours to develop. I don't strain the pani but some people do. I'll leave that up to you.

Green pani has other uses besides pani puri. Try steaming rice (see page 149) using the green pani instead of water. If you don't feel like making it, you can purchase excellent-quality green pani at Asian grocers.

PREP TIME: 10 MINUTES, PLUS CHILLING

1 large bunch of mint leaves
1 large bunch of coriander (cilantro) leaves
3 green chillies (or more if you like things spicy)
1 tsp chaat masala (see page 155) (optional)
1 tbsp ground cumin
1/2 tsp salt
1 tsp chopped ginger
1 tsp amchoor (dried mango powder, see page 155)
Salt
Chilli powder (optional)

Put all the ingredients except the salt in a blender with 250ml (1 cup) water and blend for 1 minute. If you're in a rush for deliciousness, you could add 250ml (1 cup) more water and run it all through a sieve, check for seasoning and enjoy immediately. For best results and a stronger flavour, place the paste with the additional water in the fridge for about an hour. Then run it through a sieve and check for seasoning. Add salt to taste and perhaps a little chilli powder.

Your green pani is now ready to serve. It can also be frozen for up to 3 months to use later. I always have some on hand because my pani puri parties just tend to happen late at night after a few beers with friends without any planning.

TAMARIND (BLACK) PANI

MAKES 250ML (1 CUP)

You can purchase good-quality tamarind pani (water) at Asian shops and online. It is delicious served with pani puris (see page 26). I often make my own and this is my 'go to' recipe. There are a lot of more complicated and fussy recipes out there but the end results are about the same.

Block tamarind will achieve a superior flavour but tamarind concentrate works well too and it is a lot easier. Just stir it into 1 litre (4 cups) water with the other ingredients.

PREP TIME: 10 MINUTES, PLUS SOAKING
COOKING TIME: 15 MINUTES

200g (7oz) block of tamarind or 80g (6 tbsp)
   tamarind concentrate
1 tbsp ground cumin
1 tbsp ground coriander
2 tsp salt (or to taste)
2 tsp chaat masala (see page 155)
2 tsp chilli powder
1 tbsp mint sauce
3 tbsp finely chopped coriander (cilantro) leaves
Sugar, to taste (optional)

Tamarind is quite fibrous and there are usually seeds in the block, so it needs to soak to break down the fibre and release the edible pulp. Break up the tamarind into a large bowl and cover with hot water – about 200ml ($^3/_4$ cup) should do. Let it sit for 2 hours. After this time the tamarind will be really soft. Using your hands, squeeze the tamarind until it melts into the water and breaks away from the seeds and fibres. Pass this brown tamarind water through a fine sieve into another bowl, pressing down as you do to get all of the delicious, sweet and sour pulp out.

Now add 800ml ($3^1/_2$ cups) fresh water to the tamarind water. Stir in the rest of the ingredients. This will keep in an airtight container in the fridge for at least 1 week. It can also be frozen.

TAMARIND SAUCE

MAKES ABOUT 200ML (¾ CUP)

Good-quality tamarind sauce is commercially available. It is delicious squeezed over different chaats like my aloo tikki chaat on page 16. If you fancy having a go at making your own, this recipe gets great results.

PREP TIME: 5 MINUTES
COOKING TIME: 30 MINUTES

1 tbsp rapeseed oil
1 tsp cumin seeds
1 tsp cayenne pepper
1 tsp ground ginger
$^1/_2$ tsp asafoetida (see page 155) or garlic powder
$^1/_2$ tsp fennel seeds
$^1/_2$ tsp garam masala
200g (1 cup) caster sugar
40g (3 tbsp) tamarind concentrate

Heat the oil in a saucepan over medium–high heat. When visibly hot, stir in the cumin, cayenne, ginger, asafoetida, fennel seeds and garam masal. Stir the spices around in the oil to flavour it for about 30 seconds, then pour in the sugar and tamarind concentrate along with 450ml (2 cups) water.

Bring to a rolling simmer and let the sauce reduce until it has a chocolaty colour and is thick enough to coat the back of a spoon. This should take about 20–30 minutes. The sauce will be thin but will thicken once cooled. Store in the fridge in a squeezy bottle, if you have one, and use as required. This sauce will keep for 2 weeks.

MANGO AND MINT SAUCE

MAKES ABOUT 200ML (¾ CUP)

Really good-quality mango and mint sauce is available commercially, but if you would like to make your own, it's even better. I learned this recipe from my friend Pratik Master, co-owner of Lilu in Leicester. Pratik insists on making his own and I visited his restaurant at a time when the sauce was at its best. He told me how he uses the best mangos from the Indian subcontinent but they are only in season for a short time. Look for Kesar or Honey mangos. Kesar are available from May to June and the Pakistani Honey mangos are in season around June. You can also purchase mango pulp from Asian grocers and supermarkets, which will save you the hassle of peeling and cutting up the mangos yourself. Really, any mangos can be used for this recipe but you might need to add a little more sugar to taste.

PREP TIME: 5 MINUTES
COOKING TIME: 10 MINUTES

100g (½ cup) sugar
3 tbsp mint sauce, such as Colman's
250g (9oz) fresh mango or canned mango pulp
Lemon juice, to taste (optional)

In a small saucepan, simmer the sugar with 100ml (scant ½ cup) water until syrupy. This will take about 10 minutes. Blend this syrup with the mint sauce and mango and pass through a sieve. If you find it too sweet, add a touch of lemon juice. This sauce should be quite sweet as it is normally served with and complements sour and savoury ingredients.

Store in an airtight container in the fridge for up to 5 days. I usually pour it into a squeezy bottle to decorate different chaats.

YOGHURT SAUCE

MAKES 250ML (1 CUP)

This is essentially a raita, but I call it a sauce because that's what it is referred to at many of my local kebab shops. It's that white sauce in a squeezie bottle that tastes amazing squirted all over your kebab. You must know the one? It also has sour cream in it, which I've never seen in a raita. Whatever you call it, I'm almost certain you will recognize the flavour if you frequently find yourself in the queue for a delicious kebab. Some places substitute mayonnaise for the sour cream, which you might want to try. For me though, it has to be sour cream.

PREP TIME: 5 MINUTES, PLUS CHILLING

125ml (½ cup) plain yoghurt
125ml (½ cup) sour cream
Juice of 1 lime
2 garlic cloves, crushed
1 tbsp hot sauce (shop bought or
    homemade, see page 143)
¼ tsp ground cumin
1 tbsp finely chopped coriander (cilantro) leaves
Salt and freshly ground black pepper

Place all the ingredients in a large bowl and whisk until thoroughly blended into one very tasty sauce. Check for seasoning and place in the fridge for at least 30 minutes before serving.

LEMON PICKLE

MAKES 600ML (2½ CUPS)

This lemon pickle can be made with lemons or limes. It's a simple recipe that can be prepared in minutes. You will need to wait a couple weeks before digging in though. I know it's difficult, but please be patient as the flavour is so much better. You can see a photograph of the finished pickle on the Contents page (see page 3).

PREP TIME: 10 MINUTES, PLUS FERMENTING
COOKING TIME: 5 MINUTES

4 tbsp rapeseed oil
½ tsp black mustard seeds
½ tsp fennel seeds
½ tsp cumin seeds
½ tsp fenugreek seeds
½ tsp nigella seeds (see page 155)
1 tsp black peppercorns
½ ground turmeric
2 tbsp sea salt
6 large lemons, cut into 2mm (⅛in) thick half moons
250g (9oz) piece of ginger, peeled and julienned
4 large red chilli peppers, each cut into 3 pieces
Sugar (optional)

Heat the oil in a large frying pan over high heat. When visibly hot, add the mustard seeds. When they begin to pop, reduce the heat to medium and temper the rest of the seeds and the peppercorns in the hot oil for about 1 minute. Stir in the turmeric and salt followed by the lemons, ginger and red chillies. Stir it all well in the pan, ensuring the lemons are nicely coated with all the spices.

Pour the pickle into a bowl and leave it to cool to room temperature. Taste a little of the juice. If it is too bitter, add just a little bit of sugar to taste. Don't add much as this shouldn't be a sweet pickle! Whilst still warm, transfer to a large sterilized jar with a tight-fitting lid and leave unopened for at least 2 weeks. Give the jar a good shake from time to time.

EASY CUCUMBER, CHILLI AND ONION SALAD

SERVES 4 OR MORE AS PART OF A MULTI-COURSE MEAL

You are going to love the flavours in this simple and quick salad. It is even better the next day so you can make it ahead of time and just bring it out when you are ready to serve. You can just see a photograph of the finished salad on the Contents page (see page 3).

PREP TIME: 10 MINUTES, PLUS CHILLING
COOKING TIME: 2 MINUTES

1 large cucumber, thinly sliced
1 red chilli pepper, deseeded and finely chopped
1 red or white onion, thinly sliced
3 tbsp finely chopped fresh coriander (cilantro) leaves
4 tbsp desiccated (dried shredded) coconut, toasted in a dry frying pan
Juice of 1 lemon
2 tbsp vegetable or rapeseed oil
1 tbsp black mustard seeds
10 fresh or frozen curry leaves (see page 155)
½ tsp asafoetida (see page 155)
Salt and freshly ground black pepper

Place the sliced cucumber in a bowl with the red chilli, onion, coriander (cilantro), coconut and lemon juice. Mix well to coat the cucumber pieces with the other ingredients.

Pour the vegetable oil into a small frying pan and place over medium–high heat. When the oil is visibly hot but not smoking, add the mustard seeds. The mustard seeds will begin to pop in the hot oil. When they do, add the curry leaves and asafoetida. Allow to sizzle for about 30 seconds, then pour the mixture over the cucumber mixture. Stir well and season with salt and pepper to taste.

For best results, place in the fridge to chill before serving.

CHICKPEA, CUCUMBER AND TOMATO SALAD

SERVES 4 OR MORE AS PART OF A
MULTI-COURSE MEAL

Chickpeas (garbanzo beans) just seem to go well with everything. This one can be thrown together in minutes. Canned chickpeas can be used as the recipe states, but if you want to soak and cook dried chickpeas, it will be even better.

PREP TIME: 15 MINUTES, PLUS CHILLING

400g (14oz) can chickpeas (garbanzo beans), drained
1/2 cucumber, peeled, deseeded and diced
4 large tomatoes, diced
10 spring onions (scallions), sliced
1 small bunch of coriander (cilantro), chopped
1 small bunch of parsley, chopped
125ml (1/2 cup) lemon juice
125ml (1/2 cup) extra virgin olive oil
Salt and freshly ground black pepper

Place all the prepared vegetables and herbs in a salad bowl.

Pour the lemon juice into a bowl and season with salt and pepper to taste. Drizzle in the olive oil and whisk together. Pour this over the vegetables and stir to coat. Check for seasoning and place in the fridge to chill for about 30 minutes before serving.

MIXED SALAD WITH SPICY SALT

MAKES: 3 TBSP

A few mixed salad leaves, cucumber, tomatoes and even orange wedges can look beautiful on a plate. The salad should never compete with the main ingredient of the dish but complement it.

The spicy salt should be sprinkled over the top in moderation, to taste. The recipe makes about 3 tablespoons, so you will have plenty left over for future use.

PREP TIME: 10 MINUTES

Wild salad greens or choice, including rocket (arugula)
Fresh coriander (cilantro) leaves
Baby cucumbers, finely sliced or cut into chunks
A selection of prepared fruit (small orange wedges, tomatoes and/or pomegranate seeds all look amazing)
Extra virgin olive oil, to drizzle

FOR THE SPICY SALT
2 tbsp flaky sea salt
1 tsp ground coriander
1 tsp ground cumin
1/4 tsp ground cinnamon
1/4 tsp ground mace
1/2 tsp ground ginger
1 tsp amchoor (dried mango powder, see page 155)

To make the spicy salt, mix all the ingredients together.

Decorate your plate with just enough veggies and fruit to bring colour to the dish. Don't pile it up. To finish, add a good slug of olive oil and a sprinkling of spicy salt, and serve.

TIP: You can use the leftover spicy salt as an alternative to regular salt on so many things – from fish to chicken to vegetables. It keeps indefinitely in an airtight jar, but the spices will lose flavour with time.

TURMERIC TOMATOES

**SERVES 4 OR MORE AS PART OF A
MULTI-COURSE MEAL**

I came up with this recipe one day when I
was in the mood to try something different.
I had enjoyed a similar side dish at a Chinese
restaurant near San Francisco and thought I
would give it an Indian twist. It's delicious and
adds a nice colour to the meal, too. I like to use
sesame oil in this one, but if that is too strong
for you, try rapeseed oil.

**PREP TIME: 10 MINUTES, PLUS MARINATING
COOKING TIME: 5 MINUTES**

400g (14oz) cherry tomatoes, quartered
5 spring onions (scallions), finely chopped
1.25cm (½in) piece of ginger, finely chopped
5 tbsp rapeseed oil or sesame oil
4 garlic cloves, smashed
4 cloves
4 green cardamons pods, bruised
A pinch of sugar
A pinch of salt
½ tsp ground turmeric
1 tsp garam masala
A pinch of saffron
5 tbsp white wine vinegar

Place the quartered tomatoes in a salad bowl.
Add the chopped spring onions (scallions) and
finely chopped ginger and chill in the fridge.

In a small pan over medium–high heat, heat
the rapeseed oil, then add the garlic, cloves,
cardamon, sugar, salt and turmeric. (If you don't
like biting into whole spices, count the
cardamom pods and cloves in and then back out
again before serving.) Cook, stirring, for about
1 minute, then turn off the heat. Stir in the garam
masala, saffron and vinegar.

Allow to cool slightly, then pour this mixture
over the tomatoes and stir it all up nicely. Serve
immediately, or for even better results, leave in
the fridge to marinate for about 2 hours. Stir,
check for seasoning and serve.

SIMPLE STEAMED
WHITE RICE

SERVES 4

This is the recipe I use when cooking rice for
eight people or fewer. If you are cooking for a
larger group, I recommend boiling the rice for
about 7 minutes until it is just cooked through.
This steamed recipe will, however, get you
better results. You can add spices like
cardamom pods, a cinnamon stick or whatever
you fancy to the water for additional flavour.

**PREP TIME: 5 MINUTES, PLUS SOAKING
COOKING TIME: 45 MINUTES**

370g (2 cups) basmati rice
1 tbsp butter (optional)
½ tsp salt (optional)

Put the rice in a bowl and run water over it.
Swirl the rice around in the water and carefully
pour the water out. The water will be white from
the starch. Continue rinsing in the same way
until the water runs almost clear. Cover the rice
with clean water and allow to soak for about
30 minutes, then strain.

When ready to cook, put the soaked rice,
butter and salt, if using, in a saucepan that
has a tight-fitting lid. Pour 750ml (3 cups) of
water over it and cover with the lid. Bring to the
boil, then turn off the heat. Don't be tempted
to lift the lid. Just let it sit there undisturbed for
40 minutes.

After 40 minutes, take the lid off and, using
a fork or chopstick, gently stir to separate the
grains. Do not stir too vigorously as basmati rice
has a tendency to turn to mush if stirred too
hard. Serve immediately or run water over the
rice to cool it and place, covered, in the fridge
to heat up later in the microwave or serve fried.
Please note that rice should not be eaten if it has
been at room temperature for more than 1 hour.

(< 30) (GF) (V)
VEGETABLE FRIED RICE

SERVES 4

So simple – and delicous too!

PREP TIME: 15 MINUTES,
PLUS COOKING AND COOLING THE RICE
COOKING TIME: 10 MINUTES

3 tbsp rapeseed oil, plus extra if needed
2 tbsp mixed garlic and ginger paste (see page 7)
2 carrots, peeled and finely diced
6 spears of asparagus, finely sliced
1 head of broccoli, finely chopped
2 onions, finely chopped
2 green chillies, finely chopped (more or less to taste)
$^{1}/_{2}$ tsp ground turmeric
1 tsp Madras curry powder
1 tbsp ground cumin
1 recipe quantity cold steamed rice (see page 149)
2 tbsp soy sauce or coconut amino (see page 155)
Juice of 1–2 limes
Salt and freshly ground black pepper

Heat a wok or large pan over medium–high heat and add the oil. When it's visibly hot, add the garlic and ginger paste. You are working at high heat here so continue stirring continuously so that nothing sticks to the bottom. Add your diced carrots. After about a minute, stir in the asparagus, broccoli, onions and chillies. Continue stirring until well mixed.

Now add the turmeric, curry powder and cumin and stir some more. The vegetables should be just about cooked through after another minute. You want them to still have a bit of crunch to them and not be at all mushy. Stir in the cooked cold rice. You need to stir fast but gently so that the rice is nicely coated with the oil and doesn't stick to the bottom of your pan. You can add a little more oil to the pan if needed.

Continue to fry until the rice is hot and coated with the oil and spices. Add the soy sauce and squeeze the lime juice over the top. Check for seasoning, adding more salt if necessary, and serve.

CUMIN RICE

SERVES 4

Cumin is the second most used spice in the world, second only to black pepper. So when you stopped to read this recipe, I imagine it was because, like most people, you love it. I like to serve this rice with meaty curries but it really goes well with just about anything. When I have some left over, I call that lunch the next day.

PREP TIME: 5 MINUTES,
PLUS COOKING THE RICE
COOKING TIME: 3 MINUTES

1 recipe quantity steamed rice (see page 149)
2 tbsp cumin seeds
1 tbsp butter
A pinch of sea salt

While you are steaming your rice (see page 149) heat a pan over medium–high heat and roast the cumin seeds, stirring continuously, until fragrant but not smoking. If the cumin seeds begin to smoke, take them off the heat.

Place the seeds in a spice grinder or pestle and mortar and grind slightly. We aren't looking for a fine powder here. The seeds should just be broken a bit. All of this can be done earlier in the day, but you will get the best results if done right before adding to the cooked rice.

When the rice is ready, pour the cumin into the rice and fluff it up using a fork. Stir in the butter, season with salt to taste and serve.

CORIANDER AND LIME FRIED RICE

SERVES 4

You can't beat the combination of coriander (cilantro) and lime. This recipe is one I make all the time for a quick snack. It's not just for serving as a side dish. Of course, if you want to serve it as a side, you'll be glad you did.

PREP TIME: 10 MINUTES,
PLUS COOKING THE RICE
COOKING TIME: 10 MINUTES

1 large bunch of coriander (cilantro)
2 garlic cloves
2–3 green chilli peppers
1 tbsp ground cumin
3 tbsp vegetable oil
1 recipe quantity steamed rice (see page 149),
    cold from the fridge
Juice of 2 limes
Salt and freshly ground black pepper

Put the coriander, garlic, chillies and cumin in a pestle and mortar and pound into a paste. You could also use a small blender with a little water to make this job even easier.

Heat the oil in a large frying pan, add the spice paste and fry for about 40 seconds. Very carefully, transfer the white fluffy rice to the pan with the spices. Don't just dump it in or the rice will split. Just spoon it in, a little at a time. Move the rice around in the spice oil until it is evenly coated. Squeeze the lime juice over the top and season with salt and pepper to taste. Give it one last stir and serve.

LEMON, CINNAMON AND SAFFRON RICE

SERVES 4

Lemon, cinnamon and saffron go so well together, not just in rice but in lots of different dishes. I could live on this easy, no fuss steamed rice.

PREP TIME: 5 MINUTES, PLUS SOAKING
COOKING TIME: 45 MINUTES

370g (2 cups) basmati rice
3 tbsp rapeseed oil
5cm (2in) cinnamon stick
400ml (14fl oz) can coconut milk
A pinch of saffron, soaked in a little warm milk
1 tsp nigella seeds (see page 155)
Finely grated zest and juice of 1 lemon
Salt

In a bowl, rinse the rice in several changes of water to remove any excess starch. Cover the rice with clean water and allow to soak for about 30 minutes.

Heat the oil in a large saucepan that has a tight-fitting lid over medium–high heat. When visibly hot, add the cinnamon stick and allow the oil to take on its flavour for about 30 seconds. Drain the rice and add it to the cinnamon oil, stirring to ensure the grains of rice are nicely coated with the oil. Add the coconut milk along with 350ml (1½ cups) water. Cover the saucepan with the lid and bring to the boil. When the water comes to a nice bubble, turn off the heat and let stand for 40 minutes. Don't be tempted to lift the lid.

After 40 minutes, very carefully lift the lid and stir the rice gently with a fork. If you do this too roughly, the rice grains will split and your rice will be a mushy mess, so be gentle. Just before serving, add the saffron milk, nigella seeds, lemon juice and zest, and salt to taste.

This is actually my hamburger bun recipe that I've been making since I was a kid. I've included it here because the buns are perfect served with the pav bhaji recipe on page 97. You could use any shop-bought soft buns for pav bhaji, but in my opinion it's difficult to get better than homemade. Even if you don't make the pav bhaji recipe, I hope you give these buns a try next time you're barbecuing burgers.

LADI PAV

MAKES 8 LARGE OR 16 SMALL BUNS

PREP TIME: 30 MINUTES, PLUS RISING
COOKING TIME: 15 MINUTES

2 x 7g (^{1}/₄oz) sachets dried yeast
5 tbsp sugar
90ml (6 tbsp) warm milk
2 eggs, beaten, plus 1 egg for glazing (optional)
760g (6 cups) strong bread flour
170g (1^1/₃ cup) plain (all-purpose) flour
500ml (2 cups) warm water (not too hot)
3 tsp fine sea salt

Pour the yeast, sugar, milk and 2 beaten eggs into the bowl of your electric mixer, or another large bowl if kneading by hand. Cover and set in a warm place for about 30 minutes.

When the yeast begins to foam, pour in the flours, water and salt. Stir it all up to combine, then knead, preferably with a bread hook, for 10 minutes on medium–slow speed. You can of course knead with your hands, but the dough needs to be kneaded for at least 10 minutes. You will know when the dough is ready when you take a golf-ball sized piece of dough out of the bowl and stretch it until you can see through the thinly stretched dough. At this time, the dough will be quite sticky and difficult to handle. If you are finding that you can't stretch it thinly enough, add a little water and continue kneading until you can. If you find that the dough is too wet, add a little more flour.

Cover the bowl and allow to rise for about 2 hours in a warm place. It should double in size. Punch it down and divide the dough into eight large or 16 small bun shapes. I like to press the dough balls up from underneath with my thumbs, which gives the top surface a smoother appearance.

Line 2 baking trays with baking paper. Place the buns on the trays and cover with a towel to rise for another 1 hour. (Do not use cling film/plastic wrap, as it will stick to the dough.)

Pre-heat your oven to 200°C/400°F/Gas 6. If you would like the buns to have a shiny surface, whisk the remaining egg and very carefully brush it over the buns. Do not put too much pressure on them or they will deflate. Bake for 15 minutes until the tops of the buns are nicely browned and the bottom of the buns sound hollow when tapped. Place the cooked buns on a cooling rack to cool before slicing.

I've used only a few naan recipes over the years. I found a couple I liked and stuck with them. It wasn't until I started writing this book that I really started experimenting with other options. One thing I've noticed is that curry house and takeaway naans are sweeter than the naans you find in most Indian cookbooks. They aren't sweet but they are definitely sweeter.

This recipe was sent to me by Mo Hoque, owner of the Curry Leaf takeaway in Burscough, Lancashire. What I like about it, other than the fantastic flavour, is how easily it can be prepared. You use self-rising flour so it can be used immediately, though it does get a nice sour dough flavour if left, covered to sit overnight.

Feel free to halve or quarter this recipe if you only want a few. It works every time!

QUICK ⅋ EASY NAANS
SERVES 4–6

PREP TIME: 20 MINUTES, PLUS RISING
COOKING TIME: 20 MINUTES

450g (3¼ cups) self-rising flour, plus extra if needed
150ml (⅔ cup) warm milk
150ml (⅔ cup) warm water, plus extra if needed
3 heaped tbsp caster (superfine) sugar
1 tsp salt
2 eggs, lightly beaten
1 tbsp nigella seeds (see page 155)
Ghee or butter, for brushing

Combine all the ingredients in a large mixing bowl. Knead into a soft, slightly sticky but workable dough – about 10 minutes of kneading will do the job. If you find the dough is too wet, add a little more flour. If too dry, add more water.

Cover the bowl with a damp cloth and let rise overnight if time allows. Two hours will still get good results. When ready to cook, divide the dough ball into 6–8 balls, depending on how big you'd like them. Roll them out flat. For crispier naans, you want the dough to be about 5mm (¼in) thick. Make the naans slightly thicker for fluffier naans.

Heat a frying pan over high heat until very hot. (If you are cooking over a gas flame or on a campfire, don't use a non-stick pan. I have a special treat for you.) Brush any excess flour off your first naan and brush a little water on the underside, then slap it into the pan. Bubbles will begin to form on the top just like the naans you get from the takeaway. When it is nice and bubbly on the top you can do one of two things. If cooking over a flame, simply turn the pan over to brown the naan over the fire. (This is why you don't use a non-stick pan.) If you are cooking over electric heat, flip the naan over to brown for about 30 seconds. And then flip over again and cook until you are sure it is cooked through. When the naan is completely cooked (3–6 minutes depending on thickness), keep it in a warm oven while you make the rest of the naans.

To serve, brush the tops of the naans with a little butter or ghee.

LIST OF UNUSUAL INGREDIENTS

Amchoor powder
This is dried mango powder. It is a natural way of adding a strong citric zing to many recipes. It is available at Asian shops, online and in many larger supermarkets. If you can't find it, squeeze some lime or lemon juice over the finished dish to taste.

Asafoetida
In its raw powder form, asafoetida smells terrible. Once fried, its aroma and flavour are much more pleasing, like fried onions. This spice is used sparingly as it is quite strong. In India, it is used as a substitute for garlic and onions in areas where consuming these is forbidden for religious reasons. Asafoetida is also an anti-flatulent and is cooked into dhals and bean dishes to ease digestion. Its most common use in BIR cooking is to be tempered in oil with other ingredients to make a tarka for dishes such as tarka dhal.

Bassar curry masala
This is a special spicy blend that is often substituted for chilli powder in Punjabi and Pakistani cooking. I have suggested it in a few recipes but feel free to experiment with this blend, adding it with or instead of chilli powder. Bassar curry powder is available from most Asian grocers. As this powder contains mustard oil, it shouldn't be eaten raw.

Boondi
Often used as a garnish for chaats and pani puris, boondi is small balls of fried gram flour. Boondi is available at most Asian grocers; sometimes it comes just salted but often it is sprinkled with chaat masala, which is the type I prefer.

Broken basmati rice
In recipes which call for broken basmati rice, you can substitute normal long-grain basmati. Broken rice is the rice that is broken during harvesting and processing. It is more starchy and therefore better for making dosa and idli batter.

Chaat masala
This is a spice blend like garam masala. It has a sulphuric flavour and aroma as it contains black salt. I featured a recipe for it in my first cookbook, *The Curry Guy*, but it is easily found at Asian grocers, some supermarkets and online.

Coconut amino
Coconut amino is an excellent, gluten-free alternative to soy sauce. It is popular in Indian cooking and I actually prefer it to soy sauce. It is now available in many supermarkets, Asian shops and online. The best I have found is supplied by Cocofina Coconut; see page 156.

Curry leaves
Fresh curry leaves are one of my favourite ingredients. You can find them at Asian shops, online and also in some supermarkets. If you purchase fresh curry leaves they can be frozen for future use. (Use them within 3 months.) Personally, I find dried curry leaves flavourless and a waste of money.

Fine sev
Sev is a fried noodle made from gram flour. It comes in fine and also thicker forms. Fine sev is similar in appearance to small pieces of angel hair pasta and is a popular topping for many chaats. It is available online and in many Asian shops. If you can't find it, you could substitute boondi or leave it out of the recipe.

Lentils
In this book there are recipes that call for channa dhal, black urad dhal, white split urad dhal and toor dhal (or split pigeon pea) lentils. All of these are widely available at Asian grocers, online and in many supermarkets.

Mixed powder
I have featured my recipe for mixed powder on page 49. It is essentially a curry powder and is easy to make using shop-bought ground spices.

Nigella seeds (black onion seeds)
Although often called black onion seeds, nigella seeds aren't actually from the onion family. Whatever you call them, they are excellent sprinkled over homemade naans.

Panch poran
This is Indian five-spice. There are different blends but the one used most here in the UK consists of equal measure of cumin seeds, fennel seeds, brown mustard seeds, nigella seeds and fenugreek seeds. If you have the whole spices you can mix it yourself, but bags of panch phoran are available at Asian grocers, online and in many supermarkets.

Paneer
This is the most simple of cheeses. Indian paneer is now widely available in Asian shops and in supermarkets. For the recipes in this book, commercially bought paneer will do fine, but you can also make your own. It is neutral in flavour, like cottage cheese, and comes in blocks.

Phoa
This is puffed, dried and flattened rice. It isn't used in many of the recipes in this book but it is amazing used in fried food that needs to be crispy. It is available at Asian shops and online. If you can't find it, leave it out.

Rice flour
Rice flour is gluten free and is the perfect alternative for cornflour (cornstarch). Often the two different flours are used in one recipe, but you could substitute more rice flour or cornflour if you don't have the other.

Tamarind
Tamarind is a delicious souring agent that is available in block form and as a ready-made concentrate. I use both in this book. Block tamarind needs a bit more work. You can make tamarind concentrate with block tamarind. Both are available at Asian grocers and some supermarkets.

SUPPLIERS

MEAT, SEAFOOD & VEGETABLES

Farmer's Choice
Specializing in free-range meat, sustainably caught fish and seafood and top-quality organically grown vegetables. All can be delivered right to your doorstep. I have used Farmer's Choice since starting writing my blog and they have been a valuable sponsor ever since. I can highly recommend their service.
www.farmerschoice.co.uk

SPICES, PULSES, RICE & FLOUR

Absolute Spice
I have been very impressed with the top-quality spices that Absolute Spice supply. They deliver to over 30 countries.
www.absolutespice.com

East End Foods
A sponsor of my blog for a few years, I have visited their production facilities and know I can trust them to deliver excellent-quality spices and basmati rice. I purchase whole spices to roast and grind into my own masala blends but they also supply garam masala, curry powder and other pre-ground spices that come in very handy when you don't want to roast and grind your own. East End Foods' products are available at many supermarkets, Amazon, Ocado and Asian grocers. They also have a brilliant online shop.
http://store.eastendfoods.co.uk

Plants4Presents
People often ask me where to purchase curry leaves. They are available from Asian grocers and some supermarkets. I have also had great success growing my own curry leaves from Plants4Presents!
www.plants4presents.co.uk

Spices of India
You will love shopping on this site. In addition to all the groceries and spices they supply, you will also find a fantastic range of Indian kitchen and tableware.
www.spicesofindia.co.uk

COCONUT PRODUCTS

Cocofina
Cocofina is a supplier of excellent-quality coconut products including coconut milk, coconut oil, coconut flour, block coconut and desiccated coconut just to name a few. I use Cocofina whenever coconut is called for in a recipe.
www.cocofina.com

BALTI BOWLS

The Birmingham Balti Bowl Company
Birmingham steel-pressed balti bowls come stylishly presented in a box with care guide, authentic Balti recipe and gift tag. The perfect gift for any curry lover.
www.thebirmingham baltibowlco.com

BARBECUE AND GRILLING

Thüros Barbecues
If you love kebabs, you've got to check out Thüros Kebab Grills. I love mine.
www.thueros.com

Traeger Barbecues
The easy way to get delicious smoky flavour into your barbecued foods. Traeger barbecues use wood pellets to cook the food. You can set the preferred temperature and let the Traeger do all the work. This is the perfect barbecue for easy indirect cooking.
www.thealfrescochef.co.uk/ find-a-dealer/

ONLINE SOURCES (US)

Penzeys
Large range spices that can be purchased online.
www.penzeys.com

The Savory Spice Shop
Large range of spices.
www.savoryspiceshop.com

iShopIndian.com
Groceries and Indian cooking utensils.
www.ishopindian.com

Ancient Cookware
A large range of cookware from India and around the world.
www.ancientcookware.com

INDEX

ACKNOWLEDGEMENTS

This book was a real group effort. Thank you to Sarah Lavelle for commissioning the project and to Helen Lewis and Amy Christian for all your input and work along the way. I feel lucky to have been able to work with photographer Kris Kirkham again along with his assistant Hannah Hughes. Thank you also to food stylist Rosie Reynolds for making my recipes looks so good in the photos. Thank you to everyone at Quadrille who worked behind the scenes. You understood what I was trying to accomplish with this book and your efforts are very much appreciated. I love the look of this book and would like to thank designers Smith & Gilmour for their original work in creating the eye-catching 'Curry Guy' design.

I am grateful to my wife Caroline and kids (young adults) Katy, Joe and Jennifer for being my guinea pigs when I made all these recipes at home. Thank you to my Mum and Dad, Pam and Gary Toombs, for reading the finished manuscript through, looking for typos and helping ensure there wasn't anything that needed to be edited before going to print.

For me, cookbooks are just as much about stories as they are the recipes. That's why I visit as many popular Indian restaurants as time allows to learn from excellent chefs around the UK. The following people deserve a special mention for helping me get the recipes in this book just right. Thank you Monir Mohammed from the Wee Curry Shop in Glasgow, Sabu Joseph, Head Chef of The Curry Leaf Café in Brighton, Mo Miah, from Zahmans in Newquay, Pratic Master of Lilu in Leicester, Palash Mitra, head chef of Gymkhana in London, Richard Sayce of YouTube's Misty Ricardo's Curry Kitchen, Ateeq Bhatti from MyLahore in Bradford, Vivek Kashiwale, Head Chef at Mint Leaf of London in Dubai, Tariq Malik from Al-Faisal Tandoori in Manchester, Milon Miah, Head Chef at Spice Island in Barnard Castle, Zulfi Karim, owner of Curryosity in Saltaire near Bradford. All my friends at Thali on Old Brompton Road in London, Syed Ahmed, Head Chef of Duke Bombay Café in Darlington, Alfarid 'Billy' Juma from Choma Grill House in Preston, Mo Hoque from The Curry Leaf Takeaway in Burscough, Lancashire and Shabaz Ali, Head Chef of Vijaya Krishna in Tooting, South London.

Lastly, I would like to extend my gratitude to you for purchasing my cookbook. The support that has been shown to me over the years from those who read my blog, chat on social media and purchase my books means so much to me. Thank you.

Publishing Director: Sarah Lavelle
Project Editor: Amy Christian
Senior Designer: Katherine Keeble
Series Design: Smith & Gilmour
Photographer: Kris Kirkham
Food Stylist: Rosie Reynolds
Props Stylist: Lydia McPherson
Production Director: Vincent Smith
Production Controller: Nikolaus Ginelli

First published in 2018 by Quadrille Publishing Ltd
Pentagon House, 52–54 Southwark Street,
London SE1 1UN
www.quadrille.co.uk | www.quadrille.com

Quadrille Publishing is an imprint of Hardie Grant
www.hardiegrant.com.au

Text © 2018 Dan Toombs
Photography © 2018 Kris Kirkham
Design and layout © 2018 Quadrille Publishing Ltd
Cover illustration: Shutterstock/Smith & Gilmour

Cataloguing-In-Publication Data: A catalogue record for this book is available from the British Library.

ISBN 978 178713 128 6

10 9 8 7 6 5 4 3 2 1

Printed in China

In five short years Dan took The Curry Guy from an idea to a reliable brand. The recipes are all developed and tested in Dan's home kitchen. And they work. His bestselling first cookbook – *The Curry Guy* – and the 130,000 curry fans who visit his blog every month can testify to that fact.

www.greatcurryrecipes.net | @thecurryguy